START WITH THE GIVE-ME SHOTS

START WITH THE GIVE-ME SHOTS

8 Homegrown Lessons for Business and Life

MARNEY ANDES

LIONCREST
PUBLISHING

START WITH THE GIVE-ME SHOTS
8 Homegrown Lessons for Business and Life

ISBN 978-1-5445-1870-1   *Hardcover*
        978-1-5445-1869-5   *Paperback*
        978-1-5445-1868-8   *Ebook*

For my boys, Owen and Brody

Love, Mom

and

Love always,
Grandpa John

CONTENTS

Foreword *by Lynn M. Gangone Ed.D.*   IX

Introduction   I

LESSON I: Be Proud of Where You Came From   15

LESSON 2: Start with the Give-Me Shots   47

LESSON 3: Know the Rules of the Game   69

LESSON 4: Work While Others Are on Break   91

LESSON 5: Don't Bite Off More Than You Can Chew   III

LESSON 6: Always Find a Win-Win Solution   133

LESSON 7: Tell the Truth, and You Never Have
to Remember What You Said   151

LESSON 8: What Have You Done for the Good
of the Community Today?   175

Conclusion   191

Acknowledgments   203

About the Author   209

FOREWORD

by Lynn M. Gangone Ed.D.

President and Chief Executive Officer, American Association
of Colleges for Teacher Education (AACTE), and former
Dean, Colorado Women's College, University of Denver

Marney Andes is an amazing woman.

Perhaps a book foreword does not typically open with such bold praise for the author. However, I believe telling you right away is important because I have watched her share her wisdom, light, and authentic self with so many. You'll know why I believe Marney is incredible once you read this book.

I first met Marney around 2012 when I was a college dean. Here was this woman—an accomplished professional, a former college athlete, Mrs. America, a mom, and a wife—who had also started her own nonprofit to give back to and support women returning to school to pursue higher education. Marney didn't have to add "founding a nonprofit" to her list of many responsibilities, yet she has always looked beyond her own wants and needs to be a leader who deeply cares for others and their success.

Start with the Give-Me Shots: 8 Homegrown Lessons for Business and Life gives you insight into the author and her goal—to set *you* up for success. What better way to do that than to share the authentic lessons Marney learned from her dad, a hard-working farmer and a "what you see is what you get" man, someone who cared deeply for his family and their success in every aspect of their lives.

You might say to yourself, "What can I learn from a Nebraska farmer?" Well, as someone who is Brooklyn-born and a "dyed in the wool" east coaster, let me reassure you, Marney's homegrown lessons, inspired by her dad, resonate beyond the fields of Nebraska. In fact, you'd be remiss if you don't take the time to sink into this book.

Marney has adeptly translated her dad's eight simple, core lessons for business and life—bracketed by first, *being proud of where you came from* to last, *what have you done for the good of the community*—into words that each of us can resonate with, learn from, and immediately apply to our lives.

Marney embodies the lessons she is now sharing with you. Each lesson begins with a warm story about Marney's dad and how he first taught her the lesson. Marney, the consummate coach and mentor, next transitions seamlessly from each story featuring her dad to her perspective on the lesson—its components and what she learned. Finally, by asking you to consider key questions, she shows you how *you* can benefit from the lesson. This allows you to weave your experiences into your understanding of the lessons and apply them to your benefit.

I have been a positional leader for a very long time. What makes a leader isn't position. It's trust. It's empathy. It's being your authentic self. I wish I had had this book when I first started out on my professional journey, and I am glad you have it now. These lessons will help you become the 21st-century leader this world wants and needs right now. This book allows you a glimpse into who Marney is and will inspire you to share your wisdom, light, and authentic self with the world too.

And you can thank that amazing woman, Marney Andes, for taking the time to share her dad's time-tested lessons with you.

INTRODUCTION

My last words to my dad were to thank him for everything he'd given me and to thank him for everything he'd taught me throughout my life.

He was a super-smart, hard-working farmer with a robust personality. People who knew him either loved him or tolerated him. He tended to get bigger and louder around people he *knew* only tolerated him, but those people were few and far between. For the most part, people loved him and respected the words that came out of his mouth because talking to him wasn't like talking to just anybody. When he spoke, people listened.

My dad and mom raised me, my older brother, and younger sister on a farm outside the rural community of Wallace, Nebraska, in the southwestern part of the state. For the past forty years, its population has hovered around 350 people. Wallace is the kind of place where no one locks their doors because everyone knows just about everyone else.

Our farm was located on a hill, not too far off the highway and about a mile west of town. The house sat at the very top of the hill, while the barn, livestock pens, grain bins, and a big steel Quonset (that stored tractors, tools, and other equipment) sat about seventy-five yards below. In the distance, a patchwork of pastures, corn and wheat fields, and dusty dirt roads created a crisscrossed quilt of wide-open Nebraska spaces, all of which my dad trekked and tackled on a daily basis.

My dad was a big guy. At six-foot-two, he always seemed incredibly tall to me. He inherited his prominent nose from his father, but his rugged hands and athletic fit came from working hard on the farm.

Dad mostly wore Wranglers, cowboy boots (later in life, he transitioned to Merrell's), a collared Western shirt, and a ball cap with some variety of a show steer or bull and "Monson Farms" prominently embroidered on the front.

In the summers, he always had a farmer's tan—the kind that appeared where his shirt sleeves ended. On the rare occasion when it was time to go out, Dad cleaned up nice. When he dressed in a suit, he looked more like a sharp city corporate type than a farmer.

SHOW COMB IN HIS BACK POCKET

My dad was into 4-H, a club originally created at the turn of the twentieth century with the purpose to connect public education and rural life—rural youth learned how to farm, which instilled respect for themselves and their way of life. By the time I was a kid, it had covered a wide range of activities and life experiences, but the general sentiment, focused on rural America, remained the same. Dad loved everything about 4-H. He loved the animals and the social element involved. He enjoyed being connected with people who sold the best calves with the best pedigrees. And he *really* enjoyed winning. With grand champion steers and heifers and many showmanship trophies, I remember winning more shows than I remember losing.

Those competitions were his chance to show off everything that made him incredibly proud. It was his time to shine, and his enthusiasm rubbed off on my siblings (my older brother, Cris, and my younger sister, Mandy) and me. When we rolled into a county fair (especially when we got good at competing and started to consistently win), it felt like how I imagine a professional athletic team feels when they roll into a stadium. When we arrived at 4-H shows, people knew who we were—watching us drive in and waiting to get a glimpse of us and our calves as we walked them out of the trailer.

4-H was the forum where we could all express how proud we were of where we came from, so we spent a lot of time in the spring and summer showing calves. Dad was so excited to attend (he was never more in his element than when we were at shows and the county fair), he'd speed-walk through the shows like a Tasmanian devil with a show comb in his back pocket.

When my siblings and I (and any other kids who participated) showed calves, we were expected to have a show comb in our back pocket to demonstrate good showmanship. If the judge approached you and touched the calf during competition, you were judged positively if you combed its hair back into place to create the best "showing" of the animal. Dad didn't carry a show comb for his own sake—he wasn't the one being judged. He carried it because he wanted to have it ready to help us prep the show calves or fix their hair at any moment, if needed.

When he was at a 4-H event, he moved as if time were running out, and there was quite a bit he still had to see and do. I would have fun watching and mimicking Dad's intensity because when he was at 4-H, he moved so differently than how he moved on the farm. He *could* move like that on the farm if he wanted, but it was only when something was urgent. At 4-H, he moved as if *everything* were urgent. It was an unspoken rule to let Dad do his thing and follow his lead at shows.

DAD GAVE THE BEST ADVICE

On the farm, he walked with purpose—his movements were always deliberate. If he approached me, I knew he had something specific to say. He never sugar-coated his words, and everything he did and said was intentional. He didn't hesitate to share his strong opinions with his family or with others. And although he usually couldn't be persuaded to change his mind about a topic, he would happily listen to others' perspectives and seek to understand them.

But my dad wasn't perfect. He was late to everything, and he often joked about it, saying, "I'll be late to my own funeral." He also could get pissed off, and his temper flared pretty easily. You could see it on his face and hear it in his words. There was no mistaking it, and when it happened, we would always steer clear. I didn't see it as much as others, but if a piece of machinery broke or something was going on with the family, in his mind, it was the be-all-end-all. If I were the one responsible for his anger, I would figure out very quickly how to course-correct. My dad's opinion of me mattered.

Despite his flaws and quick temper, he gave me some of the best advice through his words and example. Perhaps his first piece of counsel was, "Advice doesn't have to come from someone 'perfect.'" Everyone has flaws. If you judge someone mistakenly because of those flaws, you might miss out on hearing and taking in that one piece of advice that could be meaningful for you.

Dad took time to give me advice because he didn't want me—or my siblings—to struggle. He wanted us to be able to achieve what we wanted in life, and he wanted our journeys to be easier than his. My dad faced a lot of adversity, but it tested him, and he and my mom never backed down from the opportunity to overcome whatever challenge was thrown their way. This ability to overcome obstacles helped my dad throughout his life. His dad passed away when he was five, and he and his sister (my aunt, Karen) were raised by a single mother, my grandmother.

I can't imagine being a single mother in the 1950s. Women couldn't open a bank account or even apply for a mortgage without the signature of their husband or a male relative, just to name a *few* of the restrictions women faced back then. My grandma was a young, widowed mother of two, forced to build a life for herself and her children on her own and with next to nothing. She did it, but her circumstances (through no fault of her own) left my dad with very little when he first started out, and every step of the way, he had to fight to grow a thriving farming business. By the time he passed though, he had something to be proud of—he had amassed a herd of 600 pure-bred,

Angus cattle and, during the height of his career, farmed almost 3,000 acres of corn and wheat fields.

Dad never backed down from a challenge, and his success, especially given his background, is proof of that.

PART OF MY CORE

Dad gave us advice in hopes we wouldn't struggle like he did. Regardless of what you have to start out with, farming is hard work. Profits depend on the weather and demand for crops and livestock. For many years, especially when I was young, my dad fought to make ends meet. He wanted my siblings and me to live a better, financially secure life.

But for me, it was about more than not struggling financially—Dad's lessons were meant to help me live my life in a way that enabled me to be successful in relationships, with myself, and with others, both professionally and personally.

(My mom, Lynda, was a pivotal part of that learning process too because she shared the same values. She was an instrumental part of my life but in different ways. The tenacity and ingenuity she modeled, for example, helped lead to an amateur pageant win—more on that later—and a life-long teacher herself, she inspired me to pursue my graduate degree. I wouldn't be the woman I am today without her advice too, but I'll save those lessons for another book.)

Some of Dad's lessons I followed exactly as he suggested, when he suggested them. Others have been available to me throughout my life, but I didn't recognize them and their value until later. Some he didn't tell me until I was an adult, but each of these lessons are as important today as they were when he first shared them. To this day, Dad's words provide me direction and clarity. They have become a part of my core. Because they are applicable agnostically and relevant in every situation, my dad's lessons continue to help me grow as a person.

The point of the lessons isn't to master them, though—it's to know they're important, and that you as a human being can continue to work on the ideas represented in them to get better and improve. That alone isn't an easy feat. I grew up listening to my dad, yet each day I have to remind myself to focus on his teachings and practice them. The lessons are simple, but they aren't easy. The goal is to recognize their importance and how they can help you, and then practice them daily, so they become a part of your core too.

That's the work.

CULMINATION OF DAD'S ADVICE

Presented as eight core lessons, this book is a culmination of my dad's advice and how I have applied it throughout my life. The lessons in this book are also meant to show you how you can use them to live a more intentional, deliberate, and fulfilled life, whether in a professional or personal setting.

I have spent much of my career facilitating development for others, helping them learn a new technology, learn a new curriculum, learn about themselves, develop their teams, and develop as a leader. I've worked with aspiring leaders and executives and spoken at leadership conferences, where I have talked to leaders, including CEOs of

Fortune 500 companies. I've also coached executives and teams, given them ideas and insights, and guided them through their own journeys of discovery and self-exploration. I've seen the value in leading myself and in leading others—and my dad's lessons are always at the heart of it.

I have used my dad's lessons throughout this work and imparted his advice to the people and teams I've coached, and *these eight core lessons resonate with others almost as strongly as they continue to resonate with me.* When I went through a divorce, it was one of the hardest times of my life. I still had love for Scott, but I recognized being married wasn't the right relationship for us, which was heartbreaking. Dad's guidance, words, and these lessons not only got me through it, but they also helped me pave the right path afterward. Thanks to Dad, I was able to move on, rebuild the friendship with my ex, and shape a new life with my second husband, Allen.

My clients have similar stories and experiences as well— Dad's lessons did more than just help them get through something tough. The clients who have taken the time to learn these lessons and practice them consistently, have seen a general improvement in their lives. Now, I want to share my dad's advice with all of you. His eight core lessons are what you're going to read about in the pages of this book.

This book is not a memoir, though, nor is it my dad's biography. I'm only going to show you bits and pieces of his life, relevant to the advice he gave me. You will find real-life, practical applications of the life lessons I learned from my dad while growing up on a farm and in a small community. It's a blueprint to show you how the lessons are applicable to both your professional and personal life and how you can use them to achieve greater success.

Here's a list of the lessons you're going to read about in this book:

Lesson 1: Be Proud of Where You Came From
Lesson 2: Start with the Give-Me Shots
Lesson 3: Know the Rules of the Game
Lesson 4: Work While Others are on Break
Lesson 5: Don't Bite Off More Than You Can Chew
Lesson 6: Always Find a Win-Win Solution
Lesson 7: Tell the Truth, and You Never Have to Remember What You Said

Lesson 8: What Have You Done for the Good of the Community Today?

These lessons aren't weighed down by facts and figures, but they are tried and true. They have not only helped me throughout my professional and personal life, but they have helped others too.

Many of us over-analyze problems, over-complicate solutions, and move so quickly—bouncing from one task, event, or obligation to another—we are left feeling overwhelmed. We want to live an intentional life but don't know how to simplify—we don't know how to focus on the things that bring us joy and make us feel more complete. So many of us have manufactured a complicated environment that prevents us from achieving these things, which is why the straightforward nature of these lessons is so powerful. They cut through the noise, provide clarity, and leave you feeling grounded.

In today's over-complicated world, we need simple solutions to our problems, not complex ones. Dad's lessons deliver that. Any time I feel overwhelmed or directionless, Dad's advice gives me clarity and focus—it always realigns me. My dad's lessons have helped me navigate life's challenges and obstacles, and I will continue to rely on them for the rest of my life.

Dad was a Midwest farmer with a big mouth and a big presence. He was proud of where he came from, and you should be too. Let's get started on Lesson 1.

Dad and me at the county fair when I was too young to participate but old enough to show him I was tired of *waiting* to participate.

BE PROUD OF WHERE YOU CAME FROM

Dad wasn't from our family hometown of Wallace, Nebraska. He was from Paxton, a town about thirty-five minutes away. Both towns are small farming communities.

Mom and Dad didn't grow up together—they met as teenagers at a local dance. Mom was studying education, and Dad was studying business at the University of Nebraska, and they married following my dad's junior year and my mom's sophomore year (he was a year older). After living together for a year in Lincoln, Dad graduated and accepted a teaching position in Chadron (more on how he did that with a business degree later) on the other side of the state. At that point, my mom was a few months pregnant, so she moved to Chadron with Dad and took time off from classes to have and then raise my older brother, Cris.

Mom would have finished her degree, but Dad wasn't happy teaching in Chadron. He missed small-town living and, specifically, life on a farm. Growing up, he lived in town but would spend the weekends and summers at his grandparents' farm and was proud to do it. He loved the country and being out in the fields with his grandfather and especially loved playing with his grandparents' dogs, a love that continued throughout his life (my dad always had dogs on the farm). Dad grew up around farmers and enjoyed the small, rural community of Paxton. He had worked in "the city" for two years, didn't like it, and wanted to move back home.

So, he did. He resigned from his teaching job in Chadron and moved to my mom's hometown of Wallace to pursue a tough career in farming. (My mom's parents were farmers, and Dad believed the opportunity would be better there.) My brother was a newborn, so Mom went with him. Three years after that, she took Cris back to Chadron to finish her degree in elementary education at Chadron State College. (There's no way she could have left him with Dad, who was starting their farming business.) A year later, with my brother on her hip and her degree in hand, she was back with Dad on the farm, and there they remained for the next forty years.

YOUR BACKGROUND IS VALUABLE

My dad was appreciative of his background—he grew up with farmers and was proud to celebrate it.

I'm proud of my background *now*, but for a long time, I didn't share Dad's sentiments. For most of my teens and part of my adult life, when facing new situations away from the small farm-town life I was used to, I would look at myself in the mirror and say, "How long before people figure me out? How long before they realize I'm from a small farm town and make assumptions about me because of it? How will I be able to convince people I can take on complicated, complex problems when I've lived, in their minds, a simple life?"

The first time I recognized the value of being proud of where I came from, I was in La Junta, Colorado, teaching a small, rural community of teachers how to best use technology in the classroom. I had moved to Colorado to pursue my graduate degree, and this was my second job after receiving it. I was working as a technology consultant for a grant-funded organization that provided resources and development for teachers across the state of Colorado.

I wasn't nervous or excited when I arrived in La Junta—I was focused. I was there to do a job: guide and support these teachers while they learned a new technology.

When I introduced myself, I said something like, "Hi. I'm Marney Duckworth. I received a degree in secondary education from the University of Nebraska and obtained my master's degree in information and learning technologies from the University of Colorado at Denver. Now, I'm working as a technology consultant." ("Duckworth" was my married name at the time.)

As I taught the class, I couldn't help but notice a bunch of guys sitting in the back of the classroom who were talking amongst themselves. They weren't following directions or even participating in group discussions. They weren't interested in learning from me, and I picked up on it instantly.

These teachers weren't paying attention for two reasons: they didn't think the subject matter could help them, and they had no connection to me. They didn't know I came from a small, rural farming town and that we had commonalities. To them, I was just some instructor who drove in from Denver and knew nothing about agriculture or their small community, other than what I learned in a book or from someone else. On the surface, it seemed like we had nothing in common.

I decided right then and there that I wasn't going to let these guys off the hook. I *knew* these guys. Not personally, but I knew the type. They were ag teachers (short for agriculture) and were just like the neighboring farmers and 4-h club leaders who influenced me back home in Wallace. These guys didn't want to be stuck in a classroom "learning" how to use technology to teach their students; they wanted to be outside in the fields or in the shop, doing it their way.

During the lunch break, I walked right up to them. I was cool about it, though, and even made a joke to break the ice.

"I can tell you all are *really* loving this class and just can't *wait* to get inside the classroom and use this new technology."

I can't remember exactly, but I think one of them may have smiled.

Listen," I continued, "I know where you're coming from. I'm from a small town in western Nebraska. I was raised on my mom and dad's farm. I drove tractor and combine for my dad during many summers. I've been in agriculture, *and* I've been a teacher."

At this point, their body language shifted. It looked like I was starting to get through to them.

"It may seem like this stuff is pointless for you to learn because you don't think you'll ever use it, but what if I showed you how it would *really* benefit your students? When I was in high school, if my teachers had incorporated technology into the classroom, it would have enhanced my learning and developed my skills for the next phase of my life, whether pursuing a college degree or full-time employment."

Once I shared my background and leveraged it into information they would find useful, those ag teachers became interested in not only me but also in what I had to teach. They asked about my dad and what he farmed. Through this conversation, I learned they shared the same love for John Deere equipment as my dad—it was all they and my dad would use.

In some way, shape, or form, they knew I *knew* them, that I was a "friend," and had their best interests in mind, not an empty agenda of my own to follow. Having that information made it easy for us to connect and to relate to one another. If I had simply shared my background at the beginning of the day instead of waiting until it was halfway over, I wouldn't have wasted the morning talking to people who had no interest in learning from me.

HIDING WHO WE ARE

It wasn't until later, when I looked back on my life, that I recognized other instances where being proud of and

willing to share my background might have been valuable—for instance, when I rushed a sorority in college.
(My dad was a fraternity guy, and my mom pledged a
sorority, as did my older brother and much of my extended
family, so it seemed only natural for me to participate in
rush week.)

The point of rush week is for potential pledges to get to
know the sorority members and vice versa. I had many
sports successes and speaking achievements in high
school, which I used to connect with the sorority girls.

However, I downplayed the fact that I grew up in a small
community on a farm and, for a time, lived in a farmhouse with my parents and two siblings, where we shared
one bathroom that had a bathtub but no shower. And
because our water heater was old, many times we could
only fill one bathtub of water for all of us to use. It was
pretty gross, but it was reality.

(When I was a junior in high school, my parents built
their dream home on the farm. Since my dad was always
the last guy to go through the tub, he installed two water
heaters in the new home. Thankfully, it had multiple

bathrooms and plenty of hot water. Dad was adamant about never running out of hot water again.)

The sorority girls didn't grow up on farms, didn't grow up in small communities, and most likely, didn't share a bathtub of water with their family members. They went to schools with graduating classes in the hundreds and lived in cities with multiple outlets and resources—I graduated with a class of fifteen and lived in a town with one small grocery store and a gas station that didn't accept credit cards until well after I graduated. These girls went to the mall with friends on the weekends and with their parents on extravagant vacations. They drove cars instead of tractors and went to amusement parks instead of county fairs.

Or, at least, that's the story I told myself.

I wanted to fit in. I wanted them to think I had worth. I wanted them to give me a chance. And I was worried that if they knew who I was and where I came from (that I drove a tractor for hours during the summer rather than working on my tan), they might roll their eyes and dismiss me. So, I didn't tell them. I kept my background as close to the vest as possible.

And for what? I later found out one of my pledge sisters was also from a small farming town, only forty-five minutes away from Wallace. There were a few other sorority sisters from rural Nebraska as well. I wasted so much time and energy trying to hide who I was, and in the end, it didn't matter at all. The process fell flat. No one judged me for my background. In fact, it was just the opposite—I had judged them. I had assumed they would be unaccepting of who I was, so I didn't give them the chance to form their own opinion. I judged what their reaction *could* be and took that choice away from them.

Looking back, I wonder how many other people go through the same thing and hide the fact that they grew up poor or isolated or in a specific type of neighborhood. Where you come from does not determine your worth. I know that now. It's who you are that matters.

WHO YOU ARE TODAY

Our busy lives have left us with less and less time to connect. Human beings seek to know each other and be known *by* each other. And people connect through experiences and by sharing their lives.

When people understand where you come from, they understand who you are and see the authentic you. Authenticity is valuable because it builds trust and deepens relationships.

I saw this again during my professional career when I was in a company meeting, and we shared our backgrounds. Everyone in that meeting was successful in his or her career, but each person's background varied, from growing up privileged to growing up poor.

I found myself experiencing each person very differently after learning their stories—once I knew their background, my perception of them changed. It wasn't good or bad, just *different*. I became more patient and understanding and learned how to improve my communication with each of them. My connection with them deepened simply because my point of view changed. That's the power of knowing who someone truly is. I gained a different level of appreciation for them, and it made our business relationships better.

It's valuable to be proud of where you came from, to acknowledge both the good and bad experiences that you have had along the way. No matter how pretty or ugly your life has been, your background has contributed to who you are today. And that's a good thing.

Your background is your foundation. It's where you came from. It's what makes you, you. Your experiences in life, good and bad, don't define who you are. But they *have* influenced you. Even the bad experiences—*embrace* them. Know those experiences helped shape who you are today.

If you suppress your background and the stories about how you were brought up and how you came to be—if you don't let others see the real you, you lose out on the richness of what makes you unique. You also lose a genuine piece of what you can offer others. But when you share your background, you share the authentic you. While that's not always easy, when you're proud of who you are and where you came from (and you show others the authentic you), it's incredibly liberating.

Your background doesn't excuse poor past behavior, but it can help others understand why you are taking a particular approach to a problem or why you are behaving in a certain way. It can also help you understand the behavior of others.

For example, if you're a business leader and your family struggled financially when you were growing up, you may be more prone to making very specific business decisions in your role. Your budget-mindedness may err on the side of being budget conservative and viewed by coworkers as unwilling to spend.

If I don't agree with your decisions but know your background, I can more easily understand why you're making them—because you were always fearful about not having enough money in your life. Now, instead of thinking you're difficult to work with and unwilling to invest in a service or resource I believe our organization needs (because I disagree with you), I see the value in your background and realize you're looking out for the best interests of the company based on *your* perspective.

I value where you came from, so I value your process by which you make decisions. I may not like those decisions, but I can see things from your perspective now, so I value how you came up with them because that's who you are.

When others know your background, it enables you to:

- Connect with people
- Deepen relationships
- Be authentic

CONNECT WITH PEOPLE

When I share my background with others, people I've met in my adult life respond by saying something like, "Oh wow, I would have never known that about you," and are genuinely interested in hearing more.

For some people, understanding where others are coming from helps them get clarity. When you interact with someone and *don't* know their background, the exchange is transactional and impersonal. When you know who they are and what they're all about, the encounter becomes personal and relatable.

This reminds me of *The Wizard of Oz*. When I first watched it as a child, I was terrified of the Great and Powerful Oz. His big booming voice was so unsettling.

The picture in my mind of a big and scary being made me just as frightened as Dorothy.

But as soon as the curtain is pulled back and Oz is revealed to be an ordinary man, the perception of him changes completely. He isn't an all-powerful wizard at all—he's just a regular guy with a piece of machinery. Dorothy and the gang then find out he is only pretending to be the wizard because he thinks that's what everyone wants him to be. He thinks he has to be "all-powerful," but in the end, being himself is what gives him the connection he's looking for.

Many of us are afraid to pull back the curtain and allow others to see us for who we really are. But just as limiting is our fear of peeking behind it and seeing people for who *they* are. When we are willing to show our authentic selves and willing to look for that authenticity in others, we learn more about one another, and everything becomes a lot less scary. Being proud of where you came from isn't just about seeking to tell others details about your own life; it's also about taking the time to seek out this information from others in order to connect with them.

A lack of knowledge and connection creates feelings of fear. Eliminating fear isn't about fostering an environment where everyone is agreeable; it's about being honest with who you are and where you come from, listening to others to understand where *they* are coming from, and sharing mutual respect. We don't have to agree with each other in order to connect.

DEEPEN RELATIONSHIPS

When people know who you are and where you came from, your relationships will deepen. Knowledge of your background will help them understand how to interact with you.

Think back to that example I gave you earlier. If I know one of my colleagues is more frugal because he had an impoverished childhood, I will make an effort to provide him with extra material to support my request. I know he appreciates as much detail as possible because *I know him.* I've taken the time to ask him details about his personal life—I know what he likes to do in his free time and that his dogs are a very important part of his family.

I also know he has assumed others have labeled him as difficult to work with or unwilling to listen because he told me so. During our conversations, he's shared with me his frustration for situations where he didn't have enough detail and felt bad about denying those requests.

But he also told me he considers investments when people take the time to share more details about why the investment is needed and how it will make a positive impact. I know these details about his professional decision-making process because I took the time to ask. When I have a request, it may still be denied due to other competing investments or other influences, but because I took the time to get to know him and understand how his background influences his decision making, more often than not, my request will be approved.

BE AUTHENTIC

Being proud of who you are means being proud of where you came from. It means being authentic and your true self. And sometimes, that means being vulnerable.

Being vulnerable can be scary, but it also can be incredibly rewarding. It's an awesome feeling to be accepted for who you truly are. You can only achieve that by being vulnerable and authentic.

Authenticity has also helped me practically. Last year, I received a warning from our neighborhood HOA. It was about the exterior paint on our house. We had the house re-painted, and although the communication between me and the HOA revealed their support of the changes we wanted to make, we neglected to get specific approval for one of our accent colors. The warning, delivered via email, was a standard template and stated that they wanted us to re-do the paint job according to the colors they had originally approved. If I wanted to gain their approval for the new accent color, I would have to meet with them and "plead my case."

All of this was detailed in the warning email and created a picture in my mind of a big, bad HOA board, one that was unaccepting and unreasonable.

At first, I was fuming. I said to my husband, "This shouldn't have to be this complicated! The accent color looks great, and everyone around us agrees. We are *not* painting this house again!"

But when I calmed down and took the time to think about the situation, what I was feeling, and the role the HOA is established to play, I also remembered Dad's words—*Be proud of where you came from*—and I decided to take a different approach.

First and foremost, I checked my attitude at the door and scheduled a time to meet with the board. While I prepared, I reminded myself that, up until this point, I had never met anyone on the board. How on earth could I have any opinion of them or make assumptions of who they were if I hadn't even seen or talked to them?

And the same was true for me. They didn't know me or how important my home is to me and my family's financial future. They didn't know why I chose those colors or that others had reacted to them positively. I had never connected with the board, and they didn't have a connection with me (other than sending warning emails and knowing where I lived).

I attended the HOA meeting via a video call, and when it was my turn to speak, I told them who I was and where I came from. I told them about me, my family, and why I bought the house. I laid it all out there and held nothing back.

They shared a little bit about themselves and, lo and behold, how much they loved the colors of my house as well. That same evening, the board manager emailed me stating the warning had been dropped, and the board approved the colors on my house, as is.

I realized I didn't need to convince them to approve the paint. I just needed to connect with them.

They agreed to our request because I took the time to tell them who I was and how much the home mattered to me and was authentic when I did it. I shared personal information and showed them who I am, and they approved the new colors for our house.

REVEAL YOUR BACKGROUND

Telling others about your background can make you feel vulnerable, and for some people, it can be an uncomfortable experience. For many, that uncomfortable feeling is sparked by the concern of being judged by others. The fact is that others will judge you whether you share your background or not. Maybe you didn't have the best relationship with your family or didn't get everything you wanted growing up. Maybe you struggled in college or had a hard time landing your first job. Instead of looking at it as something negative, know that those situations, circumstances, or challenges led you to where you are today. There is immense value in that.

Imagine a life where you didn't feel like you had to cover up anything or spend any extra time or energy hiding who you are. Imagine a life where, instead, you spend that time and energy focusing on what matters. Wouldn't it be easier to live? If you don't have to make an extra effort to cover up who you are, you're free to be authentic and let others decide whether or not they want to work with you or befriend you, based on the real you.

Being vulnerable means sharing your background, so people know who you are, and sometimes that's hard. It doesn't mean only sharing your secret hopes and dreams— it means revealing insecurities and weaknesses too. Most people don't want to show others the bad parts of their lives, only the good. They want to show the world how beautiful and perfect their life is, but despite what you see on social media, no one has a perfect life. Today's world is consumed with perfectionism, but everyone has problems. Everyone has done things they aren't proud of. Sharing your background, good and bad, helps others know you on a deeper level and *connect* with you.

Whether in person, on the phone, or via social media, we are all looking for a way to connect. If leaders want to effectively mentor and lead their team, they cannot take the approach of keeping relationships an arm's length away or "business only." They must be able to connect with their team, committing both the time and effort to do so. That means being vulnerable. If parents want to better understand where their sensitive teen is coming from, they need to let their guard down, take time to listen, and be vulnerable. If you want to deepen your connection with someone in your life (professional, personal, or both), *you* need to be vulnerable.

Vulnerability can be challenging, but when you're proud of who you are and where you came from and are solid about that, sharing personal details about your background becomes a lot easier.

HOW THIS LESSON HELPED ME

As a grad student, I applied for a graduate assistant position in a technology learning lab to gain working experience and, ultimately, help pay for my tuition. The job would also give me awesome exposure—I would gain hands-on, real, applicable experience as an instructional designer, working alongside other professors, graduates, and students.

There was only one opening and many applicants, some who had already worked as instructional designers at corporations in downtown Denver. I had only taught middle school for a few years and had no relevant experience.

The interview was held on campus at the learning lab. I was scheduled to meet with the head of research, who led the work and outputs of the lab. He was a tenured professor who I had never met before.

During the interview, he asked, "Why should I hire you as a graduate assistant?"

Without any hesitation and with blunt honesty, I said, "Well, I don't have any experience. In fact, I'm guessing that I'm the person with the *least* amount of experience on all the resumes you have received. As you can see, there isn't a lot there—a few years of teaching in a middle school classroom and a deep love for using technology while doing it. That's it."

I paused before I went on to say, "But what you don't see listed on my resume—and is more important to know—is my incredible work ethic. I have within me whatever it takes to get the job done. I may not know how to do something now, but I'm a fast learner and pick up information and new skills quickly. My dad taught me how to drive a tractor, and I had no problem with that. Learning something new doesn't scare me because I've proven that I can learn just about anything. If I work with you for the next two years, I'll be like a sponge and absorb everything I can."

Then, I continued talking about my background, my home town, and working with my dad on the farm. I told

him about 4-h and my fifteen-person high school graduating class.

And then the magic of the conversation happened—the
professor opened-up to talk about his background growing up, where he completed his undergraduate degree,
and how he got into technology. He was essentially a pio-
neer in this work, doing it before anyone even knew what
it meant to teach with technology. He was both learning
and leading this work, which was exciting and challenging. He also told me that when he first got started, he too
had to be a sponge, learn fast, and work hard.

By the end of the interview (which ended up feeling less
like a job interview and more like a mid-morning conversation between two long-time friends at a coffee shop), I
got the graduate assistant job. On paper, I had absolutely
no business getting it—I got it because I made a connection with the professor. I told him who I was and where
I came from and created an environment in which he felt
comfortable doing the same.

I'm grateful I was proud of my background and shared
it with the professor. If I hadn't, I wouldn't have gotten

the job, and I wouldn't be where I am today. The graduate assistant position paid for my master's degree, which led to everything that came after it.

When I joined the workforce after the graduate assistant position, I temporarily forgot this lesson and made the assumption that people would judge me negatively if I revealed my background. I wasn't sure what they would make of it and of me, so I stopped sharing it. The risk was too great.

However, I learned from my experience teaching technology to those ag teachers in La Junta, Colorado (and over the years through various experiences), that if I want others to understand me, I must honor my background *and* be willing to share it, both the good and the bad. Only then will I be able to connect with more people, deepen relationships, and be more vulnerable and authentic.

Now, when I introduce myself, instead of only providing my educational background or my most recent job title, I say, "Hi. I'm Marney Andes. I grew up on a farm outside the small town of Wallace, Nebraska. Most of my summers were spent farming for my dad. I know the meaning of hard work. And I still work hard. I'll try anything…"

HOW THIS LESSON CAN HELP YOU

It's important to recognize that you might not be ready to start sharing where you came from. I think almost everyone struggles with this at first. If that's you, here are some tips.

When working with others, consider the following:

- How well do you know the people you work with? How well do they know you? When you know your colleagues' backgrounds (and they know yours), your relationships will deepen, and your connections will strengthen. Connecting with others leads to greater trust. And trust can lead to success. When people trust you, they are more likely to listen to what you have to say.

- If you're a leader and you want your business to thrive (and for your team to be high-performing), create *ongoing* time for them to share and get to know each other. If you don't share, you leave room for people to make assumptions about you. Don't let them assume. Let them know. Make and take the time to share and keep doing it. This isn't a "one and done" exercise. Do it continually and make it part of how you lead yourself and how you lead others.

- When you take the time to share who you are and where you came from, remember it isn't just about your physical origin—it's about your education, your childhood, experiences from other relationships, moments that brought you joy, and situations that challenged you or frustrated you.

- As you start, take pride in the act of sharing. Don't focus as much on *what* you are sharing, but rather that you *are* sharing. Good or bad, experiences have brought you to this place and have influenced who you are. There's value in it all. Just start sharing it.

- When you make time to share where you came from—as well as make space for others to share—you see others as people first, not just coworkers, neighbors, or acquaintances. Seeing the human in someone personalizes the encounter and makes it less transactional.

- Connecting with others doesn't mean getting people to like you or always agree with you. Connecting is about being real, open, and authentic. When you are, accepting someone's differences becomes easier and leads to mutual respect.

- What does your bio say about you? Does it say what you want? If not, revise it. When people ask you who you are, don't define yourself by your job title. Go back to your roots and where you came from. That is what will connect you with others.

Once you make an intentional effort to share part of yourself, it becomes easier to do so in the future. And it becomes easier for you to connect with others.

People will either like you or they won't, and that's okay. Instead of thinking, "What if people know my age or my background and judge me?", you should focus your mental energy on doing your best work and living your best life. The people you make *real* connections with won't judge you—they will see and appreciate you for who you are.

QUESTIONS TO ASK YOURSELF

How can you live authentically and encourage others to do the same? Here are some questions to think about:

- Where do you come from?
- Who and what have molded you?
- What do you value?
- What experiences in your life are most *memorable* to you?
- What experiences in your life have been the most *impactful*, good or bad?
- How did those experiences push you forward or set you back?
- Why is this story (or this part of your background) what you want people to know about you?
- How can you encourage others to share their stories?

Revealing details about yourself will help you live authentically, deepen your connections, and find more success. As soon as those ag teachers found out I was from a small farm town in western Nebraska, I earned their respect and was able to engage them in the afternoon's lessons. When the professor learned more about me as a person and shared experiences from his own life, the interaction transitioned from a job interview to a conversation, and he offered me a spot on his team.

You won't always have the opportunity to get to know someone *before* you sit down to discuss something important. That's why it's key to always carry this lesson with you. Even when others don't know your background, you do. If you've had a wonderful childhood and received all you needed in life, great. Be proud of that. If you've struggled with poverty or abuse, with school or with the law, with wealth, with family, with health—be proud of that too. You overcame a lot to get to where you are today. You should be proud of all of it.

Dad was proud to be from Paxton and Wallace. He loved small-town life, spending time at his grandparents' farm while growing up, and raising a family of his own in rural

America. Your background is the foundation of who you are, and when you're proud of it, it will be easier to live more authentically and make more connections.

While connections provide the foundation for teamwork, leadership, and success, fundamental skills matter just as much—two sides of the same coin, if you will. Dad drove this idea home time and again, as you'll see in the next lesson.

START WITH THE GIVE-ME SHOTS

"MAAAAAAAARN! Start...with...the...give...me...shots!"

My dad's big, boisterous voice rang out through the late western Nebraska morning. Each word was slow and deliberate, because he meant every syllable. He was down by the far pens, past the barn, and I was up at the driveway, shooting the basketball. He was a good one hundred yards away, but I could hear him all the same. My dad was a loud guy.

It was cloudy, like it almost always was, but for a late autumn day, it wasn't unbearably cold. That made it a good day for an outside shoot-around. Fall weather in Nebraska is unpredictable; sometimes tornado-like winds whipped around the hill where we lived and made it practically impossible to practice. But growing up on a farm meant playing sports outside, so you dealt with the conditions—you didn't let them rule you.

I paused to catch my breath and placed the basketball under my right arm. The air was crisp, tinged with an especially distinct farm scent. Smells of cedar trees, grain dust, and livestock hung in the air.

Imagining I was maneuvering cone drills in a gym, I started to dribble again, running back and forth on the driveway that was only a few years old. My dad was especially proud of that driveway—he'd poured it to provide us with as close to a half basketball court as possible, and he spray-painted it with lower blocks (the lane, or "the paint") and a three-point line. All of his children not only liked basketball but were good at it, and he was determined to give us access to the tools we needed to hone our skills.

He was also adamant about learning the fundamentals. I had just walked a few steps out of the house and onto the concrete driveway before heaving the basketball from the three-point line a number of times and only making a shot here and there.

Retrieve, dribble, shoot from the outer edges, and chase again.

After watching the ball bounce off the rim (and me scrambling to chase the rebound and retrieve the ball before it rolled off the edge of our "hill of no return" behind the backboard), my dad had enough. That was why he bothered to shout up at me from the other side of the farm.

Sound carries in the country, so there was no denying his booming voice or the lesson that we were about to revisit. On a Friday night in the fall, not only could you hear the collective crowd noises at the high school football field, but if the air was just still enough, from our porch, you could make out someone shouting, "Go Blue!"

I was still chasing after the ball when I saw my dad gunning up the hill. He was on a one-way mission, headed directly toward me with those determined steps that only came with urgency.

"You gotta start with the give-me shots, Marn," he said again and took the ball out of my hands. He was no longer bellowing the advice, but his words were still strongly stated. What he said, he always meant.

"I know, Dad," I said as I looked down at the ground and shook my head in frustration.

I wasn't negating what my dad was telling me—I was shaking my head because I was disappointed in myself. I had heard him say the same thing dozens of times, and yet he had to remind me of it once again.

"Start with the give-me shots. Once you shoot enough of the give-mes, then you can move on. Get it out of your head right now that you're too good to put the time into dink ball. You can either practice the give-mes everyday so you rule them, or you can think you're too good for them and avoid them, and let them rule you."

Dad wasn't disciplining me—he was teaching me about discipline.

My dad walked toward the hoop and stopped on the right side, straddling the lower block of the lane. He pointed down to his feet and said, "You need to take one hundred shots from here." Then, he walked over to the lower-left block, pointed down to his feet again and said, "One hundred shots from here." Finally, he made his way to the center of the lane, pointed down to his feet one last time, and said, "And one hundred shots from here." All three spots were just two feet from the rim.

"If you practice these over and over, Marn, they'll be so automatic, defenders won't be able to stop you when you take shots from inside the lane. Start with those, and then you can move out farther from the basket."

"Those shots you were warming up with?" He dismissed the idea with a heavy wave of his hand as he referred to my competition. "Let all of *them* warm up like that." And then pointing at me he said, "But you? Every time you come out here to shoot, every time you're in the gym shooting, every time you warm up before a game…give-mes."

The give-mes were the easy shots, the ones within the lane and close to the basket. The shots you shouldn't have to think too much about but what he believed too many players took for granted. They were easy points to earn but only if you put in the time and repetitions. Dad insisted that in order to have the rhythm, form, and consistency for twenty-footers or three-pointers, you first needed to master the fundamentals of "dink ball."

I met my dad's stare, looked him in the eyes, and simply stated, "Okay. Got it."

There was nothing else to say. My short break was over. He passed me the ball, stepped back so that I could take his place and, with arms crossed, stood for a moment to watch me. I took one hard dribble, spun the ball backwards and into my right hand, and started to practice my give-me shots.

START WITH THE FUNDAMENTALS

The give-me shots are what my dad considered the fundamentals of shooting basketball. *Your* give-me shots provide the foundation that makes you who you are and showcase what you do well. They are the fundamental skills that you excel in (or can even be skills you've taken for granted), and everyone's individual fundamentals are different.

One of my personal fundamentals is my ability to connect with others. Another is my knack for public speaking. My fundamentals are uniquely mine, and your fundamentals are uniquely yours.

Your fundamentals are things *you* do well, but every job, every career, and every life path has fundamentals essential to its success too. In your professional life, what are the "give-me shots" that could lead to success? Is it flawless written or verbal communication? Is it excellent attention to detail?

Whatever those fundamentals are (personal, professional, or both), practice them every day because:

- It will help you hone your best skills
- It will help you prioritize where to spend your time (on those skills)
- You will learn and build on those skills, and because of the repetition, they will come naturally to you, even when you're challenged

If I find a few days have passed and I haven't worked on my fundamentals, I redirect and start practicing them again. That's how essential they are for my success. Without the fundamentals, it's difficult to do much else.

If you're an actor, for example, you must practice memorizing your lines and work to get off book (script) as quickly as possible. Once you have and no longer have to rely on reading from the script, you're free to focus on what else needs to occur in the scene: movement, blocking, and how other actors are responding.

If you compare those who are truly successful to those who aren't, you will see it is successful people who know their personal fundamentals as well as the fundamentals related to their business *and* practice them often.

Michael Jordan made basketball look effortless. It would be easy to say he was naturally gifted, but that's not what made him great. He worked harder on the fundamentals than anyone else because he wanted to win. He practiced his give-mes every single day, and that helped him become a great basketball player.

The same principles apply to everything. Start with your give-me shots, and practice them every day.

BUILDING BLOCKS TO GROW

Individuals aren't the only ones who need strong fundamentals to grow—businesses need them too. Fundamentals are the building blocks that hold a business together. Without the fundamentals in place, it's impossible for a business to grow.

Building a business without firmly established fundamentals is like planting flowers, but instead of nurturing the plants, you fail to water them, and the flowers wither and die. You then have to re-plant flowers, over and over again, each year. (Or, because the effort may seem too big or not worth the time, you decide not to plant in that flower bed again and move on.) If you plant new flowers, however, and ensure they receive sunlight and water, the flowers will grow and bloom. Water and sunlight are fundamental to the success of the flowers, just as give-me shots are fundamental to the success of any business.

If you're a business leader, you must nurture the fundamentals until they become ingrained into your processes—only then will your business have the opportunity to grow. For example, if your company has a killer sales process, make sure every new hire is provided the resources and development needed to implement the process well and make sure existing employees receive ongoing development to do the same. When the fundamentals are in place, your business is better enabled to weather challenges (such as a recession or an epidemic) and pivot and innovate more easily.

I've worked with executives who lead large parts of the organization where they work. They each are asked to grow their businesses significantly, all the while maintaining their current portfolio. And due to the ever-expanding operation they are leading and acquiring, most have the additional challenge of supporting newly formed leadership teams as well.

While speaking with each of them one-on-one, they have shared examples in their business of what and where they want to innovate. We've discussed what they need to do as leaders to support the innovation, as well as what their teams need to do and what systems or processes need to be in place to support it.

Time and time again, the discussion of innovation always leads us back to the concept of fundamentals. I've heard statements like, "We want to engage with new technology, but we need to fully utilize what we already have," or "There is huge value in helping my team get grounded on the foundations of what we do well so that we can deal with the new challenges when they arise." I've also been told, "I know I may sound like I'm not willing to change. I am. But we've been successful for a long time, doing some very specific things well. Why do I want to disrupt that?"

Without explicitly saying it, most of the leaders I work with share the belief that building and nurturing a solid and successful foundation determines their team's and organization's success. And when they detour from the fundamentals of what makes their team or organization great, they see a negative impact.

There is a strong connection between the team's fundamentals and their ability to innovate. I've seen it in the teams I have led and in the teams of the leaders I've coached as well. My current team revisits and reinforces this concept as needed. We acknowledge and celebrate our fundamental strengths and what we are good at as individuals and as a team. In turn, we parlay those fundamentals into the services we provide and the programs we develop and facilitate for the broader organization. We've experienced first-hand how working consistently on the fundamentals (and spending the time to create a solid foundation) helps to deliver quality and impact and provides the necessary support when doing something new or reacting to change.

When COVID-19 hit, our organization needed a way to quickly help our providers and clinical teams use telemedicine to support our patients. Our ability to react quickly and effectively wasn't due to deep subject-matter expertise or past experience. In fact, we had to learn how to use the tools and learn more about the problem we were trying to solve, navigating multiple teams, resources, and processes quickly. We were able to provide a solution because we, as a team, had our foundation in place.

Every day, we work on the skills and foster a practice that keeps all of us focused on the teammate experience. We have established systems that support our approach to collaborative work. We constantly practice the skills necessary to maneuver a large, matrixed organization for the successful delivery of programs and services. Establishing a long-standing environment by which our fundamentals were in place and practiced consistently, was key to successfully and quickly supporting our organization when it needed a solution. We had committed to preparation long before COVID-19, which prepared us to deliver impactful training and resources for our providers and clinical teams. Because we practiced our give-me shots daily, we were able to deliver quickly and effectively.

If businesses focused on the fundamentals at all levels and practiced them every day (instead of *only* trying to do things that are five steps ahead of where they are currently), they would master those fundamentals, which would create the building blocks for faster growth and the ability to react in times of change and ongoing success.

INTENTIONAL TIME TO PRACTICE

In order for the fundamentals to build your business and for you to grow personally, you can't ignore the things that may seem like they are easy or second nature to you. You have to practice them every day for the rest of your life, and you *must* carve out intentional time to do so. My dad shouted up at me because he wanted me to deliberately practice the give-me shots, and he wanted me to practice them every day. For you, practicing daily doesn't mean you have to go through all twenty things you're good at. That's a lot to think about. It means picking a few skills to focus on today and a few others to focus on tomorrow. The key is to rotate what you practice, so all your skills are maintained.

In my experience, if you focus on what you do well, and you do those things consistently, you will catapult much further than you would if you *only* focus on trying to improve your weaknesses. I have seen this play out, time and time again, in my personal life and have coached my clients around similar situations too. There are some people who say, "The same things that got you where you are today won't get you where you want to be tomorrow," and I believe this can be misleading. I think growing and learning is a part of it, but you've got to nail the fundamentals and set your foundation first.

Whether you're working on a new project, starting a new job, or dealing with an intense personal issue, ground yourself by focusing on your fundamentals—what you should be able to do well because of all of that practice.

When you continue to do those things well, it sets you apart from others, and that skill becomes a unique identifier for you. If you don't practice the fundamentals every day, your skills take a hit, and you potentially lose your ability to do them. You lose what makes you unique.

HOW THIS LESSON HELPED ME

Today, it seems like practically everyone is trying to do *everything* instead of recognizing their strengths and focusing on them. They're trying to be everything to everyone.

It happens to me too. I can quickly get pulled into something and get overwhelmed by the amount of information I need to process or the number of things I need to do. But I've decided that's not where I want to be in my life. I don't want to be good at every single thing. I want to be good at things that bring me personal fulfillment, like coaching leaders and teams and speaking to large audiences. So, that's where I choose to put my energy, and

I try *really hard* to honor that. I'm not always successful, but the point is to be mindful of it and to *try*.

My professional career consists of communication, speaking, and leading and supporting high-performing teams.

The fundamentals I rely on have become my give-me shots. I work on these skills constantly, so when I have a busy or a difficult day, I can rely on them to get me through. Here are three of my personal fundamentals, things I consider I do very well:

- Presenting to others
- Telling stories that inspire action
- Helping businesses resolve issues

Let's look at how I've applied this lesson to the second fundamental—telling stories that inspire action.

FUNDAMENTAL: TELLING STORIES THAT INSPIRE ACTION

If I'm asked to speak at a conference, I craft my message around personal stories that will help explain the concept, make connections, and inspire action. I'll ask:

- What stories or examples will help the audience see me as someone they can trust and want to continue to listen to?
- What stories from my life or my experience will connect the audience to the content?
- What stories does the audience need to hear at this moment?
- What stories will help the audience reflect and naturally think of their own stories related to the topic?

I think about the stories, write key highlights noting where I was, what I was feeling, and what dialogue I may have had with others. I don't stop at simply identifying the story I want to share—I think about why the story matters and what elements of the story will be helpful and impactful. I keep the right pieces in and exclude everything that doesn't add value.

When I haven't taken the time to identify the right stories and dig into the specific details, it has left me feeling disheveled and unorganized. What if I leave important details out or, worse yet, ramble on without a clear ending? If I want my stories to make sense and have an impact, I have to practice telling them.

HOW THIS LESSON CAN HELP YOU

"Start with the give-me shots" doesn't mean you shouldn't be willing to learn something new or to work on your weaknesses. It's about helping you determine your strengths and what you do well and focusing on those every day.

If you're unable to figure out your strengths, this is an opportunity for you to ask an instructor, a coworker, a family member, or a friend for help.

You can say, "You see me do things. What do you think I'm good at? From your perspective, what appears to come naturally for me?"

If you're early on in your career—maybe you're starting out as an analyst, and you eventually want to be the chief financial officer—find someone who is at the director level or higher and ask her, "What has gotten you here? Where do you excel?" People usually know what they are good at, but if they can't clearly articulate it for you, find others who work with that person and ask them. Do this until you determine the fundamentals that led to the type of success you are hoping to achieve. Then, practice those fundamentals every day, so you become good at them. This will position you for success.

If you're hiring or supervising others, give your first-level managers the same amount of attention you give your high-potential, top-talent teammates. Everyone needs to know how to lead a team. *If you haven't developed all of your managers to be leaders, why not?* At the very least, if you must focus on top talent, work with first-level managers at the same time. If you're a leader, it's important to give everyone on your team a fair chance to succeed, and that means giving them the fundamental tools they need to do their jobs well. For managers, this means leadership coaching and the time to practice what they've learned, developing themselves as a leader, and developing their team.

Think of a new coach who is hired to lead a college football program after a losing season. He's expected to be the savior and turn the team's losses into wins. But it's bad policy to assume he will turn a losing program around in a year or two and then fire him when he doesn't. He must have time to recruit new talent and to work on the fundamentals with his new team. If he is a new or an inexperienced coach, he needs time to come into his own. Only then will the team have a chance to succeed.

The same holds true in business. If, as a leader, you're firing or demoting people before giving them time to learn and practice the fundamentals, you're doing your new manager, your teammate, your team, and your company a disservice. I talk to leaders about this all the time and say, "You can pull the plug on people, but have you made it clear which fundamentals are needed for success in the role? Have you given them the tools, resources, and support they need to be successful? If you have, have you given them time to try?" You have to give your team time to hone their skills and implement them. You have to give them enough time to succeed.

QUESTIONS TO ASK YOURSELF

How can you identify which fundamentals are unique to you? How can you determine which are necessary to advance in your career? Here are some questions to get you started:

- What are you naturally good at?
- What are the fundamental skills that have led to your success?
- What are the fundamental skills of your profession or craft?
- Who is successful in your field? What fundamentals have made them successful?
- What are the fundamentals of your business?
- What are the fundamentals of other successful businesses in your industry?
- How are you practicing these fundamentals each day? How much or how little?
- If you're not making time to practice the fundamentals daily, what do you need to move or stop doing to make room for them?

My dad wanted me to start with the give-me shots—he wanted me to practice my basketball fundamentals every day until I mastered them, and they became automatic—even at the end of the game. So, I paid attention to those fundamentals every time I went out on the basketball court, and I can't tell you how many times I relied on them to make buzzer-beaters and win. Often, during games, I'd watch others miss shots they should have made if they had put in the time and repetition needed to excel.

When given the opportunity to shoot the give-mes, I rarely missed. I wasn't shooting twenty-foot shots or three pointers—I was shooting the fundamental shots, five to ten feet away from the basket. By starting with the fundamentals and practicing like I did, not only did I score more for the team, but I was also free to focus on more advanced skills in team practice instead of being forced to focus on the fundamentals.

When I graduated from high school, I was the fifth all-time leading scorer in Nebraska girls basketball history and was awarded a full-ride college basketball scholarship. And I absolutely attribute it to my dad and his insistence that I master the fundamentals and start with the give-me shots. Dad also insisted I know the rules of every game I played. Lesson 3: "Know the Rules of the Game" is coming up.

KNOW THE RULES
OF THE GAME

The summer before my sophomore year in high school, I sat on the floor of our two-story, Nebraska Cornhusker red farmhouse (way too close to the TV) and watched Miss Nebraska introduce herself during the live, nationally televised Miss Teen USA pageant on CBS. With one finger pointed at the screen, I turned to my mother, who sat near me on the couch, and said, "See? There's obviously a Miss Nebraska pageant happening somewhere."

Mom had competed in a few pageants herself when she was younger, and she knew it was something I wanted to do too. We had been watching this pageant together for five years and had talked about it.

She nodded, her way of showing me she was listening, but her eyes stayed glued to the TV.

"I don't want to *talk* about doing this anymore, Mom. I just want to do it." Pointing to the television screen, I said, "I'm going to be there someday."

Growing up, I always watched pageants with my mom, and Dad sometimes watched with us from his recliner, which was in the back of the living room and perfectly positioned for him to see the TV. Many times, my brother and sister watched too, all of us piled in the living room together, surrounded by the combination of farmhouse wallpaper, wood paneling, and 1970s orange, brown, and mustard yellow paint that covered the walls—as well as our shared love of watching competitions, be it sports or beauty pageants.

Once I knew I no longer wanted to just watch but wanted the chance to compete in the Miss Teen USA pageant, I needed to figure out *how*. I didn't know anything about pageants other than what I had watched on television, but

Dad had always told me that as long as I knew the rules of the game, I could do anything I wanted. Plus, I had an invaluable resource—my mom. With her help, I could figure it out.

Mom's experience was limited to a few local pageants. She had some basic knowledge we could use, but the rules of those pageants were different. We needed to dig deeper to learn all the rules of the Miss Teen USA pageant game. Over the following months, she made phone calls and gathered some high-level information about pageants. The next thing I knew, Mom was driving me forty-five miles northeast of Wallace to North Platte. With a population of about twenty thousand, it was the closest "big town" and where you could find what I've always referred to as the three *M*s: the mall, the movie theater, and the McDonald's.

In North Platte, we spoke with a local florist, who grew up in Wallace (and my mom knew well) and had supported pageants in the past. He told us who we needed to contact and how to apply. He also shared tips and tricks for competing:

- **How to walk on stage:** relaxed, as if gliding across the stage, with shoulders back and a big smile

- **What to wear:** a long and beautiful evening gown, a flattering dress for the interview, a swimsuit (that would be provided by the pageant), and high heels

- **How to interview:** be ready and willing to give opinions on various topics

Although I'd never modeled or participated in a pageant, I felt confident that I could do it. Talking about myself and giving my opinions would be easy because I inherited my "gift of gab" from my dad, and I was raised by my parents to always speak freely about my opinions. I already owned a long, sequined gown that I'd bought for high school prom my freshman year, and I'd wear my "Sunday best" dress for the interview. After determining I had all the pieces necessary to compete, I didn't think too much beyond that. I was given a checklist and had everything on it. *Check, check, check.* In my mind, I was ready to compete.

As my mom and I continued to visit with the florist, he shared tales of pageants he'd been involved with and then went on to tell us about the "unspoken" pageant tips we needed to be aware of. For instance, cleavage was expected during the swimsuit competition, and most competitors used duct tape to achieve that look. I remember thinking to myself that duct tape must be known as "miracle" tape, because if it could make my (barely) size-A chest look like something heaving during the swimsuit competition, then I had overlooked the value of duct tape.

The florist also shared that I needed a way to prevent my swimsuit from "riding up," because it was a big no-no to walk across the stage with a wedgie (my words, not the florist's). Despite the "extras" we needed to be prepared for, I wasn't turned off or even *thrown* off. These were the rules of the pageant game, so I took note of them, prepared to practice them, and planned to play by them in order to be as strong a competitor as I could be.

When we got back home, we called Dad into the kitchen, and we all sat around the table while Mom and I proceeded to give him the download of what we learned about competing in pageants.

You would think that sharing tips and tricks about creating cleavage and preventing a swimsuit from riding up would make anyone's dad exit the conversation just as fast as it started…but not my dad. He was a competitor at heart, and if I was going to compete in a pageant (or anything else in life), I was going to compete to win.

He sat back in his chair with his arms crossed in front of his chest—a sign he was listening—until we finished. He paused to measure his words, and we waited, eagerly, to hear what he had to say. After what seemed like forever, he shifted his body forward, placed his elbows on the table, and held up his right pointer finger. Dad's gestures were as deliberate as his words.

"One. You aren't putting duct tape on your skin." He shook his head and chuckled. It was low and soft at first, but then it began to build as he went on to say, "If they all knew what we held together on this farm with duct tape…"

His chuckle had transformed into a full-blown laugh at this point, and he couldn't finish his sentence. But he didn't have to. Mom and I got the point.

"You can use athletic tape instead," he said when he finally stopped laughing. "At least you'll be able to remove that without tearing off half your body."

Without skipping a beat, he held up a second finger. "Two. If you need to spray something on your butt that will prevent your swimsuit from riding up, I know exactly what will keep it in place. I mean, that thing won't move. You know what you're going to use?"

He looked at me and waited. He wasn't going to give me the answer. He wanted me to realize it on my own.

A second later, I did.

"Dad, no! I can't use that on my butt! I really *will* be the country bumpkin at the pageant! Are you serious?!"

Dad was talking about the adhesive we would use on our animals—market steers and heifers—when competing in 4-H shows. (Yes, the term every beauty pageant competitor wants to think about is "heifer.") After washing the calves and grooming them, we'd brush their hair and then put livestock grade adhesive on their legs and tails to keep the hairs in place.

My dad went on to say, "If the point of it is to keep that swimsuit from moving, then you're going to use it. No one will ever know." And he was right...my swimsuit never rode up when I competed (although I remember feeling odd when I applied the same type of product to my body as we did our calves). Later, when I competed in the Mrs. Colorado Pageant and then the Mrs. America Pageant (both for married women), my dad shipped me cans of that same adhesive.

He was right again—no one ever knew. (Well, that is, until now.)

The pageant took place in Omaha, the largest city in Nebraska, which was a five-hour drive from home on east Interstate 80. As we road-tripped in our red Suburban, I practiced answering sample interview and stage questions with Mom. I took care to follow the rules and focus on the tips and tricks the florist had given me.

With athletic tape and Sullivan's Livestock Adhesive Spray in hand, I competed in and *won* the 1992 Miss Nebraska Teen USA pageant. Knowing the rules of the pageant game is what set me on the path to victory.

WHY KNOW THE RULES?

My dad ingrained this lesson in me. He told me to gather information if I didn't understand something or didn't know how something worked, so I could respond appropriately when needed.

Remember when I told you he got a teaching job even though he had a business degree? That's because he figured out the rules of the draft game. By the time my dad started college, the Vietnam War had been going on for almost ten years. Dad had seen too many of his friends come back from that war either emotionally or physically damaged (or both). He also knew a lot of young men who never came back at all. And despite having a father who fought in World War ii, my dad decided he wasn't going to go. He did a little homework, learned the rules of the draft game, and discovered that teachers were exempt from the draft. So, he took the necessary classes to obtain a teaching certificate, affording him the opportunity to accept a teaching position at Chadron High School. As a result, he wasn't shipped off to war.

(Yes, he dodged the draft, but he didn't run and hide—he

figured out what he needed to do to avoid it. And I'm happy he did because I may not be here if he didn't.)

Dad believed that nothing was too big or too difficult if you knew the rules of the game. If you wanted to play, you had to learn the rules. That's what he did with the draft, and because I knew the rules of competitive pageantry, I won on my first try.

Sports participation is an obvious example. You must understand the rules of the game to play. But surprisingly, I still find people who don't study and apply the rules before they do. They dive in head first, without first learning the rules of whatever game they're playing. I was raised in a sports-minded family, where the rules of the game are paramount, and continue to nurture that mindset with my own boys. My ex-husband, Scott, is good at this with our son, Owen, my eldest. Owen started playing competitive club baseball when he was around ten (he started playing little league at five) and still plays today. Connecting with the right clubs and coaches, who can support Owen's individual game, is incredibly important if he wants to build his skills and grow as a competitive baseball player.

Scott, who played baseball in high school and has continued to coach from time to time, has led the way. He has found the right teams and leagues to support Owen's growth, and I've been there to connect the nuances (finding a batting coach and, most recently, researching camps). The point is that none of the tools Owen has to help build his baseball skills were put there by chance. When it comes to developing our son's baseball expertise, Scott and I know the rules of the game, and we apply them to help him achieve his goals.

My husband, Allen, and I take a similar approach with our son, Brody, my youngest. Similar to Owen, he demonstrated an athletic ability early on, so we decided, when the time was right, we wanted to teach him how to ski. (Allen is a life-long skier and always dreamed of enjoying the sport with our son someday.) When Brody turned five, we decided he was old enough for ski lessons, but instead of leaving his equipment up to chance and enrolling him for classes on any old mountain, we made sure he had the best equipment and a good experience, right out of the gate. My husband tackled skis and boots (Brody was too young for poles), and I researched and talked to others to find the best ski lessons for kids.

After a conversation with a close colleague, I learned that Keystone Ski Resort had a great kids' program (It was easy to access, supported small class sizes, and served lunch.), so we enrolled him in lessons for three days. I learned how to ski on the mountain at Keystone when I was a kid—on a trip with my Aunt Pat and Uncle Bob—so it was even more special that Brody would learn there too.

After his lessons, my husband and I took over. When we went on a run, Allen would lead the way—so Brody could see him model good form—and I followed to pick him up if he fell. Everything was intentional and planned because we knew the rules of the teach-your-child-how-to-ski game.

If you want to succeed, you've got to know the rules of the game. This lesson doesn't just apply to sports; it also applies to the game of life. Everything has rules. "Know the Rules of the Game" means two things:

1. Taking the time to research and understand something before you jump in
2. Knowing that if you're willing to put in the time to learn the rules, you can do anything

When I decided to pursue my own work as an independent consultant, I initially focused only on getting enough contracts to make it. In short order, I had a solid portfolio of clients and, at one point, had to turn away good work to ensure I didn't overextend myself and be unable to deliver. When it was time to file my taxes for the first year I was self-employed, I had to scramble to assemble business receipts and documentation. The second year was even more frustrating because I brought in bigger contracts (I started to align my fees with the services I was providing) but didn't have much left over and was exhausted. So, when the long-time family accountant instructed me to do a few things here and there around tax filing time, it was a fire drill.

In my third year, when I was on my own, post-divorce, I took inventory of the situation and started asking questions. I reached out to some other small business owners to gather ideas and feedback and attended a networking event where I met a local accountant and discussed my frustration with bookkeeping and filing forms. I would later hire his firm to not only help me file my annual taxes each year but file my quarterly taxes throughout the year too. This relationship connected me with a small payroll company and other professionals who were there to advise me on how to run a successful consulting business.

Because I took the time to learn the rules of the business-ownership game, I was able to assemble a "team" of professionals who relieved me of tasks I didn't have time for nor have the expertise to complete. This new team and their implemented processes led me to revise my fees and contracts, make more money for my services, and free up time to continue to meet with potential clients and solicit new and exciting business.

DO YOU JUMP RIGHT IN?

Many people jump right into situations without knowing the rules. (I jumped into business for myself without knowing the rules, for example.) You can be incredible at your job, the best even, but without knowing the rules, you might not be able to grow and flourish like you want to. It isn't just about what you bring to the table. Not knowing the rules will hold you back. On the other hand, if you *do* know the rules of the game you're playing, whatever they may be, you don't have to be the biggest expert to win. Knowing the rules gets you more than halfway there.

If you're in a new situation and can't figure out the rules, network and connect with others. Ask a lot of questions. Be inquisitive and learn from what you hear and what you observe.

That's what we did when I wanted to participate in the pageant. My mom and I didn't know much about pageants other than what we had seen on TV. So, she used her connections to learn the rules of the pageant game. She reached out to someone she knew had the information we needed, then we asked a lot of questions. We didn't jump right in—we took the time to learn the rules from someone who knew them better than we did.

HOW THIS LESSON HELPED ME

Before me, only a handful of athletes from Wallace had been recruited by colleges. I knew nothing about recruitment and how it worked—neither did my dad, who had never been recruited himself. But I was excited about the opportunity to play college basketball.

My dad and I wanted the recruitment process to be a success. Playing basketball on a scholarship would be a huge achievement, but we didn't know the recruitment rules. So, my dad researched and learned all he could about recruitment, and when he discussed options and opportunities with college coaches, he knew what he was talking about.

He learned the rules of the recruitment game, and as a result, I was pursued by several colleges. In the end, I decided to attend the University of Nebraska at Kearney.

Today, I always apply the rules of this lesson when working in new situations, with new people, or in a new environment. I take inventory of the game so that I know how to play successfully, and I take pride in being able to do so.

For example, when I have a meeting scheduled with another leader, I think in advance about the rules and how I want to interact with them. I try to determine the following:

- What materials I may need to create
- How to present the material to them
- If I need to ask for support
- How to provide updates following the conversation

In addition, I learn:

- The rules that will govern that conversation
- What the other person expects from our conversation
- How the organization runs
- The organization's norms, if appropriate to the situation

If you don't know the rules of the game, how a leader works, or how a team functions, you're working at a disadvantage, and your chances for success are greatly reduced.

Sometimes things don't work out because there's simply a bad fit among people and situations. Sometimes someone doesn't understand what you're trying to convey. But most likely, when things don't work out, it's because *you* didn't understand the rules you needed to play by.

I'm not saying you should go into a situation and simply follow unwritten rules, no matter what. You must use them to your advantage while still being you.

There were times when I've ignored the rules or went into situations not knowing them. Early on in my career, instead of asking questions, I would rack my brain trying to guess what others wanted. At the time, I thought asking questions showed weakness or would make me look like I didn't know what I was doing, so I figured it out, all by myself.

I know differently now. Asking questions is what helps me understand the rules of the game. It's also less stressful to ask questions than it is to go in blindly to a situation and try to figure it out on my own. I try to coach everyone on my team to ask questions—and lots of them.

Those situations early in my career taught me a lot: I have learned as much through my failures as through my successes. It took me two years to win the Mrs. Colorado pageant because I didn't take the time to ask questions and learn the rules. I knew the rules of Miss Nebraska Teen USA, but Mrs. Colorado was a different animal.

Once I learned the Mrs. Colorado rules and applied them, I was better positioned to win.

Not all pageants are the same.

Not all leaders are the same.

Not all companies are the same.

You must know the rules every time you engage with someone because understanding the rules enables you to be a better competitor.

HOW THIS LESSON CAN HELP YOU

This lesson can be applied to just about everything.

Learning the rules of the game means you can stop going into a situation blindly and without knowledge. Like Dad would say, be a student of the game so that you can play your best. Observe successful leaders and teams you work with and seek to learn the rules they play by to win.

If something isn't working the way you think it should, ask yourself why, then consider what you've done successfully in the past in a similar situation and determine why it worked (or why it didn't). Now, experiment by applying those skills to your current situation and testing your findings. This could be as simple as knowing whether a formal presentation is required or as complex as facilitating a strategic business planning session.

It's also important to know the rules of someone else's game, so you can understand how they operate and better engage with them. It helps you go into the conversation with an open mind, which will enable you to grasp what is being said and navigate the situation, particularly when it is ambiguous. Knowing the rules helps put things into perspective.

This is similar to the purpose of psychometric tools or personality tests. Meyers-Briggs, DISC, and Enneagram, to name a few, are used to gain insights for individuals and teams. The person taking the assessment learns about themselves, and if used as a team-building tool, they learn about their coworkers too.

This opens the door for connection and understanding, which then creates a better working relationship. Once you know someone's results or their "rules," you can figure out how to best engage with them.

QUESTIONS TO ASK YOURSELF

Identifying the rules (and then navigating them) can help you in both your professional and personal life. Here are some questions to help you explore this lesson further:

- What are the rules of the game in this situation?
- What are the rules of the game with this person?
- What are the rules of the game with this organization?
- How are decisions made?
- How is information shared?
- Who knows the rules?
- Who have you observed playing the game well?
- How can you learn from them?
- Where can you go to learn more?

I haven't perfected using this piece of advice, although I've been in situations where I've used it well. There also have been times when I've completely failed. But I've given myself some grace when that happened. There's no way anyone can be successful 100 percent of the time, and knowing the rules of the game, in whatever you do, is an ongoing, situation-based learning process. If you use the rules to your advantage, you can't go wrong.

But rules can only get you so far. If you aren't willing to work hard, you still won't be able to win. Like Dad would always say, "You've got to work while others are on break."

WORK WHILE OTHERS
ARE ON BREAK

When I was in fourth grade, my mom learned of a volley-ball camp in Ogallala, Nebraska, a town about forty-five minutes northwest of Wallace. By that time, I had already acquired a deep love of sports and relished any opportunity I had to play.

Both of my parents came from sports backgrounds; my dad was a great high school athlete. He played quarterback and was the power forward on the basketball team, like me. He was also a high jumper and ran the hurdles—unfortunately, he missed State his senior year because he broke his arm while competing in high jump only a few track meets earlier. At the time, he held the record in the boy's 110-meter hurdles (Class D) and was expected to win State. When my mom was in high school, she was considered one of the best volleyball players in the area, so they naturally encouraged my interest in sports.

I loved my experience at volleyball camp, so the summer after fifth grade, I attended basketball camp. The age requirements stated campers had to have completed sixth grade to attend, so my dad lied about my age on the application because:

- He believed I was good at basketball
- That I could compete against kids older than me
- And that it would give me a boost to get ahead

My sister, who is two and a half years younger than me (she was a freshman in high school when I was a senior), also attended camp in the summer. When it came to camp, we were very different in our approach. Before the morning session of camp started, I would get up with enough time to shower and head to the student cafeteria to eat a bowl of cereal, while she would roll out of bed and

grab a cold slice of leftover Domino's pizza, her favorite—
but we shared the same love of sports. And now that we
knew what they were, we shared a love for sports camps.
We made great strides in our skill levels every time we
attended.

Dad always said, "Every camp you go to, every league you
sign up for, helps you change and get better. You can't just
put in the same work as everyone else and expect better
results. You've got to work while they're taking a break if
you want to be better than them." And he was right. I got
better, *faster*. My hard work was paying off.

But at some point, I started questioning whether I wanted
to continue attending volleyball and basketball camps,
playing sports during the day, and being cooped up in a
college campus dorm room at night. I had been going for
years by then, and it used to be something I enjoyed, but
now, I considered staying home, so I wouldn't miss out on
the fun things my friends were doing, like dating, going
to the movies, or spending time at the lake.

I didn't love that my dad was having me spend my entire
summer inside a gym. At times, quite frankly, I was

probably a jerk about it. Can you imagine spending all that money on camps for your child to not appreciate them?

Dad said, "Every time you go to camp, you gain a season on everyone else who took the time off, doing nothing." (For Dad, that meant anything that wasn't a summer job or working on your athletic skills.)

So, I went.

I may have been a jerk about it, but when I was younger, deep down, I loved this mandate because I adored sports in general. Once I reached high school and had a boy-friend though, I became conflicted. I still loved sports and wanted to go to camp, but I also wanted to spend the summer hanging out with my friends and (more so) my boyfriend.

In my mind, being away at camp prevented me from see-ing my boyfriend for regular dates. And this was many, *many* years before the invention of cell phones, which meant I couldn't speak to him on the phone either. (There was no way my dad was going to fund long-distance fees for idle teenager chit-chat.)

Dad said again, "Every time you go to camp, you gain a season on everyone else who took the time off, doing nothing."

I was a gifted volleyball and basketball player. Boyfriend or no boyfriend, deep down, I knew going to camp and participating in leagues was paying off because I was receiving recognition, be it MVP awards or acknowledgment from camp coaches and league organizers. I had natural talents from both my parents, and I knew I should nurture those gifts. That's why I went.

And sure enough, each summer I attended sports camps, I saw improvements in my game—far greater than my peers who stayed home for the summers. They started off the school year at the same athletic level as when they had left in the spring, while I got better every year.

Although some people have exceptional gifts that enable them to be great at something—sports, math, writing—without much practice, for most, it doesn't come easy. Even those with natural ability must work on their skills if they want to improve and learn something new. CEOs aren't born overnight—they have to work hard on their skills, for a long time, to make it to the top.

People often look at others and marvel at what they've done without knowing the work that went in to getting there. For example, they'll see someone who has left their company to start a new business and are amazed at what they've accomplished but don't understand the amount of effort it took. People don't just up and quit their jobs and instantly start their own amazing business. They have to work while others are on break.

If you want to make progress, you'll have to make sacrifices. You must work when other people take time off. It's the only way to stand above the crowd.

My mom and dad made tremendous financial sacrifices to send me and my sister to sports camps. And my sister and I made sacrifices too by not hanging out with our friends (and *boyfriends*) all summer. But we both held sports records, were all-state, had successful sports careers, and received full-ride college scholarships, all because we worked while others took a break.

GAIN A SEASON IN THE OFF-SEASON

I'm not saying to work yourself to death, to slave away at your desk for sixty to seventy hours per week indefinitely—or to do something that doesn't give you joy or to focus on something that won't help you achieve your long-term plans. That's not the lesson here.

The lesson is to *invest* in yourself, so you can thrive instead of just survive. Take time for yourself and focus on what interests you.

I'm writing this book in addition to working a full-time job and being a wife and a mother of two active boys. I could choose to go home and binge a new Netflix series with my husband. Instead, I'm investing in myself and building on the skills and lessons I've learned to make myself a better asset at work and to the world at large.

I'm trying to gain a season by working in the off-season.

I've heard so many friends and colleagues talk about how they dislike their current jobs or the type of work they do for a living. Yet, they don't put in the time to make a change. They work forty to fifty hours a week and then go to happy hour, rest at home, or play on the weekends before going back to do it all over again. I understand they're exhausted, but the weekend (or weeknights) is the time when they could be working on something that gives them true joy or puts them on a better path.

Put into perspective the extra time you spend working toward accomplishing a goal. Whether it's a one-day training or a six-month certification course, that will give you a boost in your career, the extra time you're spending is finite—it is one moment in time, not your entire life. It's a small strategic move that leads to something greater. "Work While Others Are on Break" doesn't mean you put in the extra time until you retire. It means you put in the extra work where and when it counts.

And that move enables those who make it to get ahead of those who don't.

If you want to be the person who gets ahead of others, you're going to have to work harder than the majority of people. That doesn't mean to throw your life away in the process, taking class after class for the next twenty years.

But maybe, for the next six months, you can take that programming course and get certified because it will elevate your career.

If you want things to change, you must make sacrifices.

BALANCE YOUR TIME

I love when people, especially women, ask me, "How do you balance it all?"

I tell them openly and honestly, "I don't. The time I put into my work while people are on breaks is a trade-off, but I'm committed to the potential gain on the other side."

There are times when I suddenly try to figure out how to balance my time, such as when one of my boys is playing a game across town on a Saturday (or even more challenging—when they both have a game at the same time and at two different locations in town) and I need to prep a presentation for an early morning meeting that coming Monday. Do I stay home to prepare, or do I go to the games? This decision is difficult because I will only have a certain number of opportunities to attend my boys' games.

If I don't go, I disappoint my boys and miss out on an opportunity to spend time with them. This may impact our relationship. They might think I like my work more than I do them, which I imagine would be hurtful.

If I go to the games, I'm possibly risking career advancement or losing my livelihood. That presentation might put me on the path toward a promotion or give me the experience I need to take on a stretch assignment when I want to. (A stretch assignment is a project beyond the scope of your current role that gives you experience or helps you build skills to prepare you for more advanced roles.) If I screw it up, I could be evaluated poorly and passed over when the next opportunity presents itself.

The hard truth is you can't have it all—you have to pick and choose. That's where a lot of people, especially women, get into a rut. They want something and don't know how to get it without disappointing others. Or they try too hard or work too much in an attempt to make everything happen at the same time.

It's important to focus on the right things. What will get you the results you want? I started my charitable giving organization, Project Aspire, in 2006, and in 2013, I wanted to expand it. (Project Aspire funds scholarships for women in the state of Colorado who are pursuing higher education degrees.) There were many weeknights and weekends I had to dedicate to learning about nonprofits and how to draft the documentation and forms necessary for obtaining 501c3 status. I had to give up quite a few games and time with my family to meet with nonprofit experts and consultants to help me achieve my goals for the organization. I had to make sacrifices.

If you don't want to disappoint your child, go to all of his games, spend time with him after work, and look for activities you can share together on the weekends. Put progressing in your job on the back burner. If you want that promotion at work, work hard while at the office and put in the extra time you need to stand out among your colleagues. This will mean spending less time with your family.

You've got to be the star of your own movie. It's not about doing what everyone else tells you to do. It's about doing what you need to achieve success.

HOW THIS LESSON HELPED ME

When my mom and dad picked camps, they researched them first to determine the best fit for me and what I needed to get out of it. If I was going to sacrifice my freedom during the summer to play volleyball or basketball, the sacrifice needed to be worth it.

My dad's advice about working in the off-season wasn't simply a generic statement. He meant that it was important to work while others were on break, but strategically. It doesn't mean over-working yourself at just anything—it means setting an intentional goal with a specific timeline.

For me and my sister, that meant sports camp when we were kids. Throughout middle school and high school, we worked while others were on break. It was a set timeline with a definitive goal—college scholarships—and it paid off. I played basketball at a Division II school, and my sister played all four years of Division I volleyball for the University of Nebraska.

Professionally, before meeting with other executives, I've spent many late nights perfecting a presentation to ensure I communicated my team's ideas to the best of my ability. I've also prepped and dress-rehearsed the flow and transitions for team development sessions, so I could deliver a great experience. And I continue to meet with other coaches and colleagues to help me think through what I need to do as a leader; how to engage my team, support them, and lead the way so that my team can do their best work. I believe the extra time and commitment to doing my best work has led to my success as a leader in learning and development (L&D).

I'm writing this book while others are at their children's games, hiking in the mountains, or watching movies. But when I'm finished writing, I'll have something to show for my effort. I will have achieved a goal.

HOW THIS LESSON CAN HELP YOU

Be strategic about how you put in that extra time. Otherwise, you will work hard for no reason at all—you'll end up breaking yourself without anything to show for it.

If you're working all the time because you're chasing a promotion or want to get ahead, you need to step back and reevaluate the specific things you want to accomplish and create a detailed list of the steps you need to take to do it. You need to think about the amount of time it will take to reach your goal and what the trade-off will be. What will you have to sacrifice?

If you're thinking you don't have extra time to work while others are on break because you (maybe) have children who want your attention, consider whether someone else—a coach, a friend, a spouse or significant other, another parent—can take your child to their soccer game this weekend. Can you put your kids to bed earlier, so you can work after they go to sleep or put in the work before they wake up in the morning? Can you work one weekend day while others are off? Everyone's situation is different, but it's important to decide how *you* plan to work on your goal—whether it's creating a business plan with your new partner or learning new skills that will enable you to change jobs—and then set aside the time to work on it. You don't have to work seventy hours a week. Carve out a specific amount of time that seems reasonable for you to work toward your goal.

I have a friend who is a mom and who also works at a very busy and demanding job. When she gets home most nights, she's exhausted. I told her, "If you want to get out of that company, you're going to have some pretty tireless nights maintaining that job while working toward another one. But if you don't work toward getting that other job, guess what? You're stuck where you are. That's just the way it is."

If you're looking to change jobs, you need to make time to:

- Determine the type of jobs you might want
- Craft a resume that highlights the skills and experiences that are important to the roles you're interested in
- Put out feelers to see if anyone knows of any jobs that might interest you
- Research available jobs online and apply to those that are of interest
- Find someone, especially with recruiting experience, who can review your resume and provide feedback

If you're looking to start a business, you need to make time to:

- Determine what type of business you want to start

- Find someone who has started their own business
- Spend time with the aforementioned person, if possible, while others are on break
- Figure out and start taking the steps you need to build your own business

Each of these steps takes time, but if you want to change your circumstances, if you want your future self to look back and say, "Man, I'm glad I did that," you have to work hard to make those changes happen.

If you put your effort and time toward the change you seek, it will give you the best opportunity to achieve your goal. If you know and acknowledge what you'll have to choose between to accomplish that goal, you're less likely to be surprised and thrown off track or distracted.

Remember, trade-offs are inevitable. I've done it for sports, I've done it in my professional career, and I've done it in my personal life because you can't do everything all the time, and you can't be everything to everyone.

I work with a lot of women on this very challenge in particular because they feel like they need to get everything done. But that's not true. I used to think that way; however, I quickly found out it isn't possible. I remember the first time I missed one of Owen's baseball games: I thought I was going to die. I thought I was a terrible mother, but then I talked to him about it and about the project I was working on, and I promised I'd attend his next game, and he understood. I also shared with him *why* I was working on the project and investing my time—my extra time and effort was spent helping women in the community pursue their degrees and supporting them financially. I told him not as a means of gaining acceptance or accolades, but because I wanted him to learn this lesson as well. I went as far as to invite him to join me at one of the fundraisers for Project Aspire, so he could see first-hand where I was spending my time. During the event, I remember he turned to me and said, "You're in charge of all of this? Wow, Mom. That's so cool."

I talk to both of my sons about this lesson and model it for them because I want them to know there will be a time when they will need to make trade-offs too and that doing so isn't a bad thing. They simply will need to be clear about what the trade-off entails and communicate that to the important people in their lives.

Acknowledge what will still need your time and attention when you work while others are on break. For me, it's my husband and sons, my family, and close friends. When I was working on Project Aspire, they all took a temporary back seat.

Working while others take breaks and choosing how to use your time most effectively isn't easy. You'll feel conflicted, especially at first, but accepting that necessity will help you weather the difficulties you may encounter along the way.

QUESTIONS TO ASK YOURSELF

Getting ahead, making a change, or starting something new means trade-offs and sacrifices. Here are some questions to help you determine how and what you need to get started working while others are on break:

- What do you want to advance in?
- What actions will help you get there?
- How much time is required to take those actions? How much time daily/weekly/monthly?

WORK WHILE OTHERS ARE ON BREAK

- How long will the additional workload last?
- What other obligations or commitments do you have that will conflict with the additional time you're committing to this new activity?
- How will you handle missing out when you have to choose?
- How will you communicate that choice?

When you work hard while others are taking a break, you have an opportunity to learn, grow, and get ahead. My dad taught me this valuable lesson back in fourth grade, and I've applied it to business, family, and life in general ever since.

But it's not just about finding the time to up your game, get ahead, or pivot to do what you love. Making those kinds of changes often has a monetary cost tied to it. We'll look at getting a handle on your finances in the next lesson.

DON'T BITE OFF MORE THAN YOU CAN CHEW

After graduating with a degree in secondary education, I took a job teaching eighth-grade social studies at Raytown Middle School, an inner-city school in a southeast suburb of Kansas City, Missouri. Home to the Kansas City Chiefs and the Kansas City Royals, it was also just minutes away from Worlds of Fun and Oceans of Fun, an amusement park visited in the summer by many Nebraskans. Raytown School District was a diverse district when I taught there and continues to be today.

The job paid $24,000 per year, and with Mom and Dad's help, I found an apartment near the school and moved in. (Given my low salary and the school district where I worked, I later discovered many of my students lived in the same apartment complex.) Prior to making the seven-hour drive from Wallace to Kansas City, we visited Nebraska Furniture Mart, where I picked out a bed, kitchen table, and living room set that my parents were kind enough to pay for and have delivered. At a nearby Walmart, we bought basic, starter appliances, which my parents also purchased for me.

My parents bought those items for me, not as handouts, but because they didn't want me to go in debt in order to have what I needed.

When it came time for them to drive back to Wallace, Dad said, "Now, let's be clear—I'm not a checkbook for you, nor will your mother and I bail you out if you get into any financial trouble you could have avoided. This is a gift to get started on the right foot. You're a college graduate and a smart young woman. Don't be stupid with your money."

I nodded to show him I understood because I did. I knew Mom and Dad didn't have unlimited cash lying around so this gift wasn't easy to give, but I also knew I wouldn't be able to fund my new life without their help.

My parents could have told me to get a loan in order to purchase what I needed. Or simply go without.

Instead, they said, "We want you to be on the right side of your future," which meant not starting off my career and adult life in debt. I was very grateful, both for the financial help and the sound advice.

Throughout my life, Dad deliberately repeated his lesson about money. All of Dad's lessons were important and present throughout my life, but this one, he made a point to hammer home with me. That's how important he thought it was. Whenever my dad and I talked about money, he reminded me, "Marn, you never want to put yourself in a situation where you can't sleep at night or where each morning when you wake up, you want to roll over to the edge of the bed and puke because you're in so much debt you can't stomach it."

Don't bite off more than you can chew. Don't buy the house you can't afford. Don't go on vacations you can't afford. Don't buy clothes and other things you can't afford.

That doesn't mean we can never spend money. My dad bought things, and I buy things. In fact, I know I've bought things that some people might look at and ask, "Why would you spend money on that?"

For example, Allen and I really like a clean car, so we have a monthly car wash membership. I love flowers in the entryway of my home but can't stand the fake stuff, so we buy a fresh arrangement each week.

There are a dozen other things I spend money on that some might consider frivolous, but I can do that, as long as I don't bite off more than I can chew.

You can buy things you want too, as long as you don't bite off more than *you* can chew.

DO YOU REALLY NEED THAT?

When I was a young adult, my dad imparted an interesting financial view.

For the longest time, he said, "You shouldn't buy a house. Always rent or lease. That way, you don't have to worry about fixing things like a broken hot water heater. That's the landlord's issue. You just put in a ticket or whatnot, and it gets fixed."

I'd say, "Oh, come on, Dad, you own stuff. Are you telling me I should never buy a home?"

To him, the choice was to own a house and go into debt or *not* own a house and *not* go into debt, and it was easy for him to decide which path I should take. But it was just a protective mechanism for him. He didn't really believe I shouldn't buy a home—he simply feared my siblings and I would buy something we couldn't afford and would struggle financially.

He never wanted me and my siblings to make financial decisions that crippled us. I suspect it's because he lost his dad when he was young, and my grandma worked for every penny to support him and my aunt, Karen. He grew up not having a lot, no father figure to provide additional guidance, and then went on to farm during lean times in the '70s and '80s, which were pretty hard years for farmers. His life wasn't easy.

After seeing how his mother struggled to provide for him (and struggling himself), he wanted to ensure my siblings and I never had to confront a financial crisis or feel burdened by finances. He didn't want us to suffer.

And this thought process continued well into my adult life. When I talked to him about buying a different home or buying something for my existing home, he'd hit me with questions like, "Do you really need that? Or do you just want it? If you lose your job tomorrow, can you still pay for it?" His questions cast enough doubt that I would take a day or two to reconsider, and many times (if not most), I realized it was a want, not a need, and I'd move on.

I took his questions and consideration to heart. My dad didn't believe his children had to be rich—he just didn't want us to waste money we might need for something else later on. He didn't want us to have to go into debt when it could be avoided.

LOOK AT THE LONG GAME

Don't be married to your house, your job, your investments, or your bills. (If you already are, it's time to make a change.) If you put yourself in a financial situation that would collapse if something went wrong—you lost your job, got divorced, got injured, or fell ill—you'd be in big trouble and wouldn't have the financial means to survive.

Look at the long game when it comes to your finances and be mindful of what you may want in the future versus what you may really need. That doesn't mean you can't buy things, treat yourself from time to time, or go on vacations. It means you won't tie yourself to something you can't get out of. Being mindful of your finances now will give you financial freedom in the future.

For the past ten years, I have made very specific and intentional financial decisions that give me the following peace of mind: if I ever lost my job, I could piece together funds, taking whatever jobs I could find, such as waiting tables as I did in college, graduate school, and early in my career, and still pay for my life. (Even with Mom and Dad's help to get started in Kansas City, my teaching salary didn't give me enough money to fund my basic life, so I got a job serving tables at night and some weekends at a restaurant near the ballpark.)

Or, if I determined my job was no longer a good fit for me or supported the career I wanted, I could afford to walk away and figure out my next step. I know it wouldn't be easy, and I certainly would need to make a number of adjustments to my current lifestyle, but I also knew it was possible, all because I wasn't trapped, financially.

A few years ago, I did just that. I was the head of talent management for a publicly-traded company, was paid nicely, and had equity but left when I realized my new boss and I had fundamental differences in the way we worked and the long-term vision we had for the company. It was hard to walk away from the salary, the security, and the colleagues I had developed strong connections with, but it was possible because I had spent my adult life practicing my dad's lesson about money. I could afford to walk away because I hadn't bitten off more than I could chew.

The freedom of knowing your finances won't bury you if something goes wrong is a powerful feeling. Not only does it help relieve stress in times of crisis, focusing on the long game provides you the ability to safely start over, if and when you need to.

SMALL CHANGES MAKE BIG IMPACTS

When you see your friends or family spending money, it's easy to get caught up in wanting to spend money too because you don't want to miss out on dinners, gadgets, vacations, or the latest trend. You don't want to miss out on buying that big house or new car like they did. But do you need any of those things? Can you really afford those things?

I'm not telling you *not* to buy something if it's what you want, but a smaller home, for example, might be more practical. Maybe it's better to buy a modest home and contribute the extra money to your child's college fund or your own retirement fund. If nothing else, it takes less time to dust. (I say this because almost everyone in my immediate family considers dusting to be the worst part of cleaning a home.)

If you go out a lot, take numerous vacations a year, drive expensive cars you can't afford, or have other discretionary expenses and find yourself in a tight financial situation, it's important to develop a financial plan. Ask yourself, "What is most important to me? What do I *need* to support the things that are most important to me?"

Is buying a daily drink at a coffee shop necessary? A daily five-dollar drink adds up over time and uses money you could put toward other expenses. Maybe you can treat yourself to coffee shop drinks once in a while instead of every day and brew coffee at home the rest of the time.

Do you eat out every day at work? Do you have to? Perhaps you can take your lunch the majority of the time, utilizing an occasional lunch date with close colleagues as a means of connecting and celebrating together, rather than eating another burrito bowl at your desk. Purchases like these, which seem small in isolation, add up quickly. If you're spending money on these seemingly small things but not saving money every month, such as contributing to a 401(k) (should you have access to one available to you through your employer) or, at the very least, putting money into a savings account, then you really do need to check yourself, and *hard*.

Making small changes to your finances can help you reach your long-term goals. When you group small spending habits into a collective whole, you can better see and feel the totality of your spending. It's easier to feel the impact. Without making small changes, your goals will be out of reach.

If building up a vacation or a college fund or paying off a car loan is a goal of yours, *now* is the time to make the necessary changes to see that happen. Not next pay period, next month, or next year...*now*. For a major financial impact later, make small changes now, and within two weeks, I bet you won't even miss what you've changed.

What small changes can you make to get you to your goals?

Whatever they are, commit to them now.

WE ALL MAKE FINANCIAL MISTAKES

For the longest time, I loved to shop. More accurately stated, I loved to *buy*. As a consultant, whenever I met with clients, I dressed to the nines, and in my early thirties, I acquired a deep love (or lust) for designer clothes and a deep need to have a lot of them. Dresses, blouses, jeans, shoes, you name it—I had to have it. Sometimes the decision to buy was spontaneous, and other times it was because I wanted just the right look for an upcoming engagement. Regardless, within just a few years, I had created a bulging closet of dressy, overpriced, and expensive clothes, many of which I barely wore.

Then, I found myself with a new job at a small tech company, the kind that provides ping pong tables as a way for employees to take brain breaks and other perks like a fully stocked kitchen, catered meals throughout the week, and a relaxed dress code. So relaxed that funny vintage T-shirts and flip-flops weren't reserved for laundry day. For this company, they were the norm.

In an instant, my closet full of fancy clothes became completely useless. Although I barely wore the clothes socially or on the weekends, now I wouldn't even be able to wear them for work. My new career move turned my expensive clothes into money collecting dust in the corner of my bedroom closet.

HOW THIS LESSON HELPED ME

I've taken this lesson to heart. It isn't exceptionally easy to practice and requires a lot of discipline, but once I implemented it into my daily life, I started to see the benefits.

One of the biggest examples of this was when I bought my current family home. At the time, the realtor told me I qualified for a much higher mortgage than I was considering. As tempting as it was to take out a larger loan and get a bigger, fancier house, it scared me. I didn't want to bite off more than I could chew. I knew the value of the lesson my dad taught me, and I wasn't going to make a bad decision that could come back and haunt me. At the time, I was a newly divorced single parent and owned and operated my own consulting company, which was the sole means of my financial stability and, most importantly, the financial stability of my firstborn son, Owen. I had healthcare, food, and other bills to consider. If I were to suddenly lose a major contract, I wouldn't be able to pay for everything.

Because I purchased a home below my means, I didn't have to worry about losing a contract. It would've been painful to lose it, that's for sure, but it would have been *more* painful if that lost contract impacted my financial stability and ability to provide for my child. Because I took out the smaller loan, no matter what happened, I knew I would still be able to sleep at night and that I wouldn't wake up in the morning sick to my stomach.

This lesson has helped me focus on what I want, which has driven my financial decisions for the better part of the past decade.

- I want a home that is paid for
- I want to have a place on the beach, where I can retreat, write, and retire
- I want to pay for my children's education and help them start their adult lives, just as my parents helped me
- And I want to do all of this without having to work until I'm in my late sixties

I have achieved the first two "wants" and am working, writing, and continuing to make financial sacrifices, so I can realize the second two. My parents believed in helping my siblings and me, whether that meant supplementing our undergraduate degrees or assisting us with whatever we may have needed when we started out as young adults. This principle has been ingrained in me, and I will pass it along to my boys. That means creating a plan to help us save for college now and avoid a big hit in the future. It also means being extremely diligent, so I can retire in my early sixties. Saving little bits today will give me financial freedom tomorrow.

My partnership with Allen also supports what I want out of life. He's always been mindful of the small expenses and how they can add up over time, and while his frugality was a bit frustrating (if not downright annoying) at times during the first few years of our marriage, it influenced me over time. A financial advisor by trade, he's a stickler on the small changes and habits needed to build a solid financial foundation, like eating in, researching the best deals, and avoiding spontaneous purchases, just to name a few. He keeps us on track and disciplined in the day-to-day, and I contribute to our financial partnership by focusing on the big wins and big investments and making a competition with myself to see how quickly I can pay something off.

Now, I think of this lesson every time I want to buy a new outfit or give in when Owen, now a teenager, begs incessantly for a Starbucks Frappuccino. And for the last eight years, to help me stay focused on achieving my goals and getting what I want, I've used questions like: *Do I order dinner for delivery just because I've had a long day? Do I continue to keep that gym membership I don't often use (or worse yet, don't use at all)? Do I parlay all of these expenses over the next few months and make an extra payment on my home mortgage? Or, do I switch gears entirely and put it all into my sons' college funds?*

This lesson has helped me make sound decisions that have put me in a good financial situation, rather than a financial emergency or crisis. When I make financial decisions, I wake up feeling good about them.

HOW THIS LESSON CAN HELP YOU

When you position yourself to have debt, you create obstacles that prevent you from following the other lessons in this book. When you're tied up trying to figure out your finances and are perpetually sick to your stomach, you can't think straight. That stress creates a challenge for every other part of your life. Following this lesson removes those obstacles.

Let's say you desperately want to leave your job. If you're in debt, that could be impossible. But if you don't bite off more than you can chew, you can create financial freedom and leaving is much easier. First, determine your goals and what you want. How are the daily, weekly, or monthly choices supporting (or sabotaging) your goals? Then, make small changes. Small changes can have a huge impact on reaching those goals.

Another bonus: when you reduce the amount of time you have to spend thinking about how you'll pay for everything, you will create more room to live and enjoy life.

When you consider making a large purchase, think about the future ramifications. Think about whether the debt you take on will prevent you from having the money you need for something else down the road. If you are buying a house, consider purchasing one that costs less than the maximum you can afford. Then, determine how soon you can pay it off. The same level of scrutiny should be applied when considering a new car. Instead of buying something brand-new, give some thought to used car options.

Think about your financial situation in the long-term, rather than what you think you might need right now:

- Take inventory of your expenses
- Determine what each expense is doing for you and how it improves or hinders your life
- Consider if each expense is necessary
- Focus on what you need as opposed to what you think you are supposed to have
- Figure out how you can have more financial freedom; that might mean moving somewhere cheaper or cutting expenses by eliminating the cable bill or not stopping for take-out coffee each morning on your way to work
- Remove the obstacles you can control

When you don't bite off more than you can chew, you have more capacity to give to others. That's another bonus. Dad was very generous—he loved to give. At dinners out, my dad would often pick up the bill, and we all knew he and my mom weren't the wealthiest couple at the table.

But my dad didn't care about that. He wanted to take care of people, and the financial freedom he created allowed him to do that. Dad gave back because he made space for it financially.

QUESTIONS TO ASK YOURSELF

You may have heard someone use the term "financial freedom" and go on to share that it is one of the most powerful gifts you can give yourself. This is true, but too often, this concept is used to try to sell you on a new investment opportunity or get-rich strategy. I'm asking you to think of the term differently—as a driving force to evaluate your life, what you spend your money on, and why you're spending it.

Here are some questions to dig into:

- What is in your financial control?
- What isn't in your financial control?
- What do you want your financial future to look like?
- Is this purchase a want or a need?
- Are you making this purchase because it's convenient?

- Is there a less expensive alternative?
- How does this purchase add value to your life?
- Does this purchase help you achieve the financial future you envision?

I'm not saying you can control everything. Circumstances may change, and you may not have the luxury of asking yourself those questions. You might get laid off. There could be a recession. You could get injured or get sick and be forced to quit your job. You may not have a choice when it comes to taking out loans.

That's a painful situation.

But if you remove obstacles you *can* control now, you position yourself so you can potentially avoid putting yourself into a financial bind. Don't plan out of fear. Instead, take inventory of your life and start making changes to better position yourself financially. And if you make wise financial decisions today, you'll be set up for life.

Now that you know how to create a winning financial situation, it's time to talk about finding win-win solutions when you're working or negotiating with others.

Let's get on with the next lesson: "Always Find a Win-Win Solution."

ALWAYS FIND A WIN-WIN SOLUTION

Just after Scott and I had agreed to the final details of our impending divorce, I visited my parents with Owen, who was six at the time. It was his fall break, so I thought it would be a great opportunity for him to get away from the disruption, play with the dogs and cats, and just be.

Owen has always been my Steady Eddy—he doesn't show a lot of extreme emotion. The divorce didn't seem to distress him, but I thought it would be a good idea for him to get away anyway. And I knew he loved the farm. He and my dad had a special connection, and Dad would often meet me halfway between Wallace and Denver and take Owen back to the farm with him for several weeks at a time.

While we were there, my dad needed to pick up a piece of equipment that was being repaired in town, so I jumped into the pickup and joined him on the drive to the mechanic's shop. During the short ride, Dad talked about how frustrated he was with the mechanic. He had given him a lot of business over the years and would continue to do so if he'd consider giving my dad a break on the cost of the repairs. The mechanic was charging more than what my dad knew he would pay at neighboring towns, but Dad wanted to give his business to the local mechanic. In his mind, it was simply the right thing to do for the community.

Now, though, my dad was at the tipping point in the business relationship. He had compromised for a win-win solution for some time, but from his perspective, the mechanic had not. And my dad had finally had enough.

When we arrived, Dad grabbed his checkbook from the dashboard and said to me, "This won't take long. You can wait here, if you want."

I stayed in the pickup and admired the familiar backdrop of downtown Wallace and the string of businesses that lined Main Street—a bank, a bar, a café, and an old theater that hadn't been open for thirty years. Not much had changed since I was in high school.

After just a few minutes, Dad came walking out and loaded the repaired equipment into the back of the pickup truck, and we started home. He was calm and level-headed when he told me about their conversation on the drive back.

Dad had said to the mechanic, "I want to make sure that you're absolutely positive this is what you're going to charge me to fix this."

The mechanic went on to explain to Dad that the price was the going rate for the repair and that he was firm on the cost and what he expected for payment.

Dad said, "I'd like to keep doing business locally with you. Are you positively sure this is what you're going to charge?"

The mechanic said, "Yes."

Dad wrote him a check and shook his hand. He didn't tell him off or storm out of the mechanic's shop. He never spoke ill of the mechanic. In fact, he never spoke of the incident again. In his mind, it was done. He had already gone through the emotions of being angry with the mechanic and had made the decision to treat the situation as a win-win. The mechanic's decision to charge my dad the full amount for the repair was the final straw—that's why Dad asked the mechanic about the charge *twice*.

Once Dad finished telling me this story, he said, "That's the last check I'll write that mechanic. I'll never do business with him again."

And my dad was firm on that. Writing that last check and walking out the door was his closure. He never again did business with that mechanic.

TWO POSSIBLE SOLUTIONS

From my dad's perspective, the mechanic was taking more than he was giving, and it wasn't fair. When the mechanic refused to charge what my dad considered a fair price, Dad signed the check and then walked away. He didn't cause a fuss because, to him, it was important to carry the win-win mentality through to the very end. How you choose to show up *and exit* matters. Creating fairness and a win-win solution also means you're fair when severing ties. Dad modeled that with his interaction with the mechanic.

In that exchange, my dad taught me there are two potential solutions to any given situation. You can either look for a win-win solution, or you can simply walk away from the situation if you don't see a means to make it fair. In a win-win solution, you both compromise to mitigate the conflict at a place where it's best for both parties. That means you're asking them to give up something, and you're doing the same as well.

This isn't about meeting perfectly in the middle, though. More often than not, the win-win isn't that black and white. Finding a win-win solution is about what makes the most sense for both parties involved in the long run. Achieving your ultimate goal in the long term may mean taking hit after hit in the beginning. Be open-minded and willing to compromise, but be ready to walk away if the terms of the deal don't work for you.

This isn't about being a giver versus a taker, either. A lot of people think it's better to be a giver than a taker, but there are positive elements to both. The first step is to discover what's fair and a win-win for both parties. Sometimes that means you have to give a little more, but other times it might mean you have to *take* a little more.

How do you discover what's a win-win? First, you need to put yourself in the other person's shoes. What's the win for them?

I don't know if my dad looked at it from the mechanic's perspective. Maybe the mechanic had been taken advantage of in the past. Maybe he didn't know how to communicate with my dad. Maybe Dad was a pain-in-the-ass client and wasn't worth the effort. What was the situation like for the mechanic?

Look from the outside in. Remove yourself from the situation, so you can see it from all angles. Figure out the win for the other party, then figure out the win for you.

When you know the win for both sides, you can determine what's fair.

You may not like what you have to do, and you may decide not to do it, but at least you understand why you made the choice and how it can impact others, so you can move on.

Sometimes you only have to give a little for a situation to become a win-win, and sometimes you have to give more. If you think what you're being asked to give is too much, you have to be willing to walk away. This is especially true if it's impossible to find a win-win situation, such as a relationship gone bad.

Once you've made your decision, don't complain about or over-analyze it. The situation occurred, you made a decision, and it is what it is. If you're unhappy with the outcome, learn from it, and don't make the same mistake again.

After that final exchange with the mechanic, Dad moved on. He didn't even tell the mechanic it was the last check he'd ever write him. A lot of people would be tempted to hold a grudge, but my dad knew that wouldn't do him, the mechanic, or anyone else any good. For Dad, it was over and done with the moment he signed that check.

A WIN-WIN MENTALITY

Growing up, I saw this lesson exemplified in other ways. For example, when someone provided my dad with a good connection to buy livestock, Dad would do things for them in return. He could have easily invested his money and time into his farm, but he didn't. He would pick up the bill at dinner or help them move a piece of farm equipment instead.

In small communities especially, nobody thinks about the transactions because they aren't always written out on paper with dollar amounts. There's plenty of contracts and leases in place, and there's money exchanged, but a lot of small-town communities create win-wins without expecting anything tangible in return. That's what Dad did. When I was growing up, many families wrote checks to the local church, but in addition to writing checks, my dad also donated his time. Whenever the priest needed a ride to the weekend basketball game, for example, Dad would pick him up and take him.

When you build relationships, you can come up with win-win situations more easily. You know who you can trust and who you can count on. This is a lesson that flourishes in small towns, and a lot of city neighbors would benefit from this simple lesson as well. My dad was the kind of person who assumed others would be there when help was needed or if someone was in a jam because he was the guy who provided that for others. It was a win-win situation born out of building relationships.

Too many times as adults, we're self-centered, constantly taking from others and negatively impacting those around us. Or we go to the opposite extreme and constantly give to others, letting people walk all over us. Neither approach is great because someone is always on the losing side of the equation.

A win-win mentality is about being fair. It doesn't mean that every time you compromise, you meet in the middle. It means that, over time, you'll work toward what both parties feel is fair in that particular situation. If you work toward what is fair, both parties will have a win-win experience. My dad knew that and built all of his relationships around it.

If, despite your best efforts, the other person always wins, you now must decide if the relationship is worth staying in, or if you should leave and stay true to yourself and your needs. Are you willing to accept the consequences of the "loss"? What would happen if you do? Or is it time to determine this relationship is not for you and you should walk away from it?

Dad was willing to walk away from his long-time relationship with the local mechanic because he no longer believed the situation was a win-win. He tried to negotiate with the mechanic, but the mechanic shut him down, so the relationship ended.

A lot of people don't know when to walk away from a no-win situation. They hang on until the bitter end.

But knowing when to walk away is empowering. It simplifies a difficult decision.

It's also a litmus test. Working toward the win-win will help you determine who to keep around, invest in, and have a relationship with down the road—and who to walk away from.

HOW THIS LESSON HELPED ME

I was thirty-eight when I gave birth to my youngest son, Brody. He is Allen's first child and my second (and together, we decided, our last), which made it a really easy decision to take the time to enjoy my maternity leave with him and be thoughtful about how and when I was going to return to work.

While making plans to return, we decided we were going to interview and find a nanny to care for Brody, at least until he was old enough to start preschool. Through a referral, we were fortunate to find an incredible nanny, Emilia ("Emmy," and eventually, when Brody began to speak, he called her "Me"—short sound for Emmy). Overtime, Emmy, who was married with three grown daughters of her own, became part of our family. The care she provided Brody, as if he was her own son, was just what we'd hoped for. She also cared for Owen when he returned home from school and took him to and from activities or other appointments as needed.

While working for us, Emmy expressed interest in Allen's car, a 2005 Nissan Altima that we were considering selling in order to buy a bigger vehicle. Now that we had an additional family member, we needed more room for transporting people and equipment for activities. Allen had researched the Kelly Blue Book value for the car, and we already had some local interest through a few one-on-one conversations. But Emmy was very interested in the car and was in need of it—her current vehicle was no longer reliable, at least not consistently.

We talked with Emmy about options for buying the vehicle and, in the end, settled on a price and payment plan that allowed her to have the car immediately. Over the next few weeks, when we paid her on a Friday, we simply deducted the agreed-upon payment amount. We could have charged more if we had sold it to someone else, but this was an opportunity to create a win-win solution. Emmy acquired a car that she was excited and proud to own for a reasonable price. For us, we off-loaded a vehicle and were able to purchase a bigger one in its place, which we needed anyway. We also had the peace of mind knowing Brody's nanny had a reliable vehicle. We weren't just selling a car; we were continuing to build a relationship with our son's caregiver.

Emmy was already committed to our family, but after this, she became the main person we could count on. When we came home later than anticipated from work (which was often), Emmy would flex for us as needed. Our win-win solution wasn't fifty-fifty on paper—it wasn't an even split. But it was fair. It was a win-win solution.

HOW THIS LESSON CAN HELP YOU

In the corporate setting, if you're always taking and not giving, get ready because no one will want to work with you.

Consider the other person. They're thinking, "All I'm doing is working myself to the grindstone, and I'm getting nothing in return. This person is a jerk."

Where is the win-win for the giver in this situation? There isn't one.

On the other hand, if you're always a giver—if you work and work and work, constantly bending over backward to give of yourself and never receiving anything in return— you probably feel taken advantage of. That's not a win-win situation either.

For example, employees are often asked to take on extra assignments as part of their jobs. They feel they must say, "Yes" to the assignments if they want to keep being employed. When an employee can't follow through and execute their tasks because they take on way more than they can deliver and are not able to do their best work, this is a no-win situation for them. It's also a no-win situation for the employee's manager and company stakeholders.

Does this sound like you? If it does, before agreeing to take on additional work, you should evaluate:

- What is being asked of you
- What you are trying to achieve if you commit to this assignment
- What you are willing to sacrifice if you take on this assignment
- The importance of the relationship to you

- In general, the types of things you agree to take on

If you're already in a no-win situation and you want to turn it around, you must:

- Decide how long you are willing to stay in that kind of relationship
- Brainstorm solutions
- Determine which solutions will lead to your desired outcome
- Enact those solutions

This same concept applies to teams and leading them. If you're a leader, over-committing your team can lead to stretching them too thin and could jeopardize their ability to deliver. This will put you and everyone on your team in a no-win situation.

QUESTIONS TO ASK YOURSELF

Finding the win-win solution in your professional and personal life can work as a framework by which you can determine if a situation or relationship is still right for you.

You can also use it to build trust. Consider these questions to help you navigate your win-win solutions:

- What does a win look like for you?
- What does a win look like for the other party?
- How much do you need to give to achieve a mutual win?
- If you need to give more than the other person, will the extra you give provide a bigger win for you down the road?
- How does this relationship serve your needs?
- What would cause you to walk away from the relationship?
- If you both need to walk away, how can you part ways and each maintain your dignity?

When a win-win situation isn't possible—which does happen—determine if you are willing to sever the relationship or live with it. My dad felt taken advantage of by that mechanic, so he decided to take his future business elsewhere. He knew when to walk away.

Most of the time, solutions exist that will benefit everyone involved. Find them. But if you can't come to an agreement you believe is fair, either now or in the long run, it might be time to follow in my dad's footsteps and break off the relationship.

The real win-win is finding a balance between giving and taking. Be a champion for your work. Develop relationships that foster win-win situations. Above all, be honest with yourself about where you're willing to compromise and change and honest with the other party about what you'll give and what you'll accept. The next lesson revolves around telling the truth. Let's dive in to what my dad said about it.

TELL THE TRUTH, AND YOU NEVER HAVE TO REMEMBER WHAT YOU SAID

One night, while I was in grade school, my parents were out for the evening, and true to form, Cris, Mandy, and I decided to run wild in the house and mess around in the living room, which had two entrances—one, outside the kitchen and the other, near my dad's office. This created a loop between the dining room and the living room.

My brother was chasing my sister and me, and after running many loops through the living room and then through the dining room, Mandy tucked herself into the loveseat while I decided the best way to get away from Cris was to jump into Dad's brand-new recliner (as fast as I could) and recline it. My thinking was that once I was in the chair, my brother couldn't keep chasing me or tackle me because the chair was an obvious "safety zone."

I took the corner as fast as I possibly could, jumped into the chair, and quickly reclined it, just like I had planned. When I looked up, my brother was flying through the air, his arms and legs spread wide, WWE-wrestling, belly-flop style. It was almost like he was moving in slow motion, and the sound coming from his mouth was low and muf-fled, like in the movies. I knew it was going to be bad, but there was no time to move or get out of the way.

When he landed, the chair made a low, deep THUD—it was an awful noise. I don't know if it was a spring that popped or something else, but at that moment, when Cris and I heard that noise, we both knew we were in big trou-ble. (Mandy was five at the time, and we knew we were responsible for her. She wasn't going to take any heat for this.) We gasped and looked at each other, our eyes wide open with dread. We knew we had broken Dad's recliner, and I was terrified of the consequences.

We peeled ourselves out of the recliner and quickly tried to fix it—we pushed the lever down and shoved the footrest until it was tucked back in. Not knowing what else to do, we sat down in another part of the living room and started watching TV.

When Mom and Dad came home, none of us said anything about the recliner, not even Mandy. The next night, Dad sat in the chair, and when he went to recline, the back of the chair dropped, and he practically tumbled backward out of the chair and into the wall behind him. The momentum nearly flipped him into a backward somersault.

My siblings and I watched as Dad struggled to get up and out of the chair, mumbling under his breath the whole time. I didn't want to look, but I couldn't take my eyes off him and his struggle with the dysfunctional recliner. None of us could.

When Dad finally got up on his feet, he looked at all of us, one by one, and said, "What happened to my recliner?"

We were frozen. We didn't look at him, and we didn't look at each other—our eyes stayed glued to the floor. We

START WITH THE GIVE-ME SHOTS

didn't say a word because we didn't want to get into trouble. We didn't want to be punished.

After that, he muttered something else under his breath and walked away.

We didn't want Mom and Dad mad at us—more so Dad, of course. Mom would typically listen to our stories and maintain her display of disappointment. Dad, on the other hand, didn't want the details. He wanted to know who did it and how it happened, so he could quickly direct his notorious question of "What the hell were you thinking?!" to the guilty party.

Discovering who broke the recliner became a big thing in our house. Mom and Dad brought it up from time to time throughout our childhood, trying to elicit the truth. But we never owned up to it.

TRUTH IS SIMPLE

Dad always said: "Tell the truth, and you never have to remember what you said."

— 154 —

But because my siblings and I didn't follow this advice when we broke Dad's recliner, we had to remember to lie for decades.

Remembering lies is complicated. It may seem complicated to tell the truth too, but often, the truth is much simpler than it seems it might be. If either my brother or I had told the truth, our conversation may have gone something like this:

> Dad: "What happened to my recliner?"
>
> Me: "Cris and I broke it."
>
> Dad: "What were you doing?"
>
> Cris: "We were screwing around."
>
> Dad: "Okay, how are you two going to solve the issue we have here?"
>
> Me: "We're not going to mess around in the house anymore. It's not a playground, and your recliner isn't a toy."
>
> Cris: "We'll do extra chores for you until we can pay to get your recliner repaired or buy a new one."

If we had that type of conversation—if we had owned up to it, Mom and Dad would still have been disappointed, but the truth would've been out there. Dad would've said something like, "I just got that recliner and didn't even get a chance to enjoy it," and then he would have told us we shouldn't run around like that or treat other people's things like they're easily replaceable. Finally, he would've sent us to our rooms to think about our actions, and the next morning, Cris and I would've come down, apologized, and came up with a plan to pay him back. We then would have moved on.

But because Cris and I didn't come clean, it was torturous for me, knowing we had broken the recliner and hadn't told the truth and admitted to our mistake. The longer our silence carried on, the more guilt I had, knowing I should have just told the truth about what had happened to the chair on the day we broke it. But instead, I tried to avoid getting into trouble at all costs, and I had to live with the guilt.

And to make matters worse, my dad kept that recliner for years—I believe, in part, because we didn't have a lot of expendable funds floating around to buy a new one. But I also believe my dad hung onto that recliner as a way to silently torture my brother and me. If that was his intention, I'm telling you, it worked. It was like that recliner had eyes that looked at me and a voice that called to me from across the room. Just the presence of that recliner created ongoing guilt for me.

Reflecting on the situation, it was also pretty obvious they knew. During random conversations or in front of others when we had company over to the house, Dad would say things like, "Man, it would be nice to have a comfortable recliner to sit in, wouldn't it? Well, I've learned I can't keep nice things around here. When you live with a bunch of jackasses who run around and break everything, it's hard to keep anything in decent shape."

Eventually, during a holiday dinner, a few years before Dad died, and when my brother, sister, and I all had kids of our own, we told Mom and Dad the full story of how the recliner broke, and they confirmed they already knew it was us; they just didn't know *how* it happened.

Everyone had a good laugh at the story then, but it represented years of hiding the truth.

Looking back, I think about the worst that could have happened. I would have been in trouble, but guilt wouldn't have eaten away at me for years. Sure, I would have disappointed my parents, but they already knew what we'd done. I expect I disappointed them even more by not telling the truth.

BE ACCOUNTABLE

Telling the truth isn't easy because there's a fear of what will happen to you if you tell someone you made a mistake. We often create our own stories about how we think people will react to our truth. We consider numerous possibilities, and most are usually negative.

When I talk to people about this lesson and being accountable, I say, "What's the worst thing that could happen? Picture that in your mind. Now, go to the opposite extreme. What is the *best* thing that could happen?"

The worst thing may actually be that you could get fired. But the best thing could be that the manager respects that you are willing to admit you need assistance or more time to complete the project, forgives you, and gives you the resources and time you need.

Honesty is hard because it is difficult to be vulnerable. But like I always tell my team, "Speak up and speak often." A lack of accountability leads to a chain reaction of problems. If you know you're going to miss a deadline, communicate that as soon as you can *before* you miss it. Don't stay silent.

If I'm working with my team and we're not approaching something in the manner the business or *my* manager expects, I'll say, "I've got some tough news to share. I know my manager wants to see it this way, and I need your help to get it there. How can we start to craft it that way?"

I don't ask questions in a round-about way. I'm direct and to the point, telling them what I know to be true.

I could say, "Well, could you try it this way?" or "What if we did it this way?"

But what good would that do? Not admitting the problem, not holding yourself accountable, or avoiding speaking your truth causes bigger problems—others are likely to react to it more negatively when they, ultimately, discover the truth about the situation.

If you speak your truth, you may say what people don't want to hear. You may even make admissions you wish you didn't. But the longer you go without speaking the truth, the harder it becomes. Telling someone that you screwed up when it happens is much easier than telling them six months or a year later.

Leaders can struggle with this because speaking the truth sometimes can be perceived as harsh, unemotional, or uncaring, but it's actually endearing and creates trust within relationships. It may be hard for others to hear, and it may not give the recipient the answer he wants, but there are positives too. Telling the truth:

- Makes you accountable for your present and past actions in that particular moment
- Puts you in a much better place because others know where you are coming from and where you stand—no one will have to imagine what's happening in the moment
- Enables you to screw up, admit your mistakes, learn from them, and fix them
- Allows everyone to start figuring out how to move forward

When you don't speak the truth and hang on to that burden too long, you are not permitting the other person to decide if they can trust you anymore and have a relationship with you. You aren't letting yourself or the other person decide whether or not your relationship is a win-win relationship because you've decided not to tell the truth.

And not telling your truth is stressful. Like it did with Dad's recliner, lies end up eating at you.

ENVIRONMENT DEVOID OF TRUST AND ALLEGIANCE

In order to get what they want, some people purposely don't tell the truth, and they don't realize it impacts others around them.

While at a previous company, my team and I had worked for a better part of a three- to six-month period creating a leadership development strategy to help support a substantial organizational change. This meant providing a foundational program to approximately forty-five existing managers and twenty-five new leaders to help them explore their roles and how to effectively lead teams. During this same time, my former leader exited for another opportunity, which left me navigating a relationship with a new supervisor.

My new boss had a different personality and adhered to a management approach I wasn't accustomed to—my previous leader was upfront and open about both internal and external business decisions. It was very much a partnership with my previous leader. With my new boss, it wasn't. This became obvious during a meeting we had with the president of the company to talk about implementing the leadership strategy I mentioned. During the meeting, my boss told the president she'd hired a consultant to develop the strategy the company was going to use for the organizational change. It was the same task I had been assigned.

I was completely blindsided. Receiving new information in the moment was both shocking and, quite frankly, unnerving. I didn't care that my boss hired a consultant, but I was put off that she didn't tell me about it *before* the meeting with the company president. It completely negated all the work my team and I had done.

Not to mention, it put me in the position of either going with the flow (of what my boss had seemingly presented to the president ahead of time) and completely negating all of the hard work that my team had accomplished, or taking a stand and asking for the president to also consider the original plan I was prepared to share. It created an uncomfortable situation, which ended with the president asking me to set up a time for a small focus group of leaders to experience what both my team had been working on and the plan my boss had discussed with him—to use her specific consultant.

Talk about being uncomfortable. If my new boss had simply been truthful with me about her plan, the meeting with the president would have been much less awkward. Plus, trust would have been established, which would have strengthened our new working relationship. Instead, we started off on a dishonest foot.

And that wasn't the end of it. My boss and I went on to host a leadership development program "dance off" (as one of my teammates jokingly referred to it) and gathered feedback. The focus group chose the plan my team had been working on, not the plan the consultant presented, yet my boss offered him a contract and brought him into the organization anyway. Again, this wouldn't be a problem, but she wasn't truthful about that either. My boss didn't tell me about this decision ahead of time. Instead, I found out after all the paperwork had been signed.

Within a few months, I decided to exit the organization. It wasn't an easy decision (and I did it without a new job lined up) but one that had been made clear. I liked the company's mission, purpose, and possibilities, but I couldn't continue leading good work if I felt it wasn't supported in an honest manner. I could no longer work for someone who didn't practice this lesson—the way my new boss conducted business wasn't going to work for me because it wasn't a win-win. If you cannot speak the truth, you create a no-win situation and an environment that is devoid of trust and allegiance.

HOW THIS LESSON HELPED ME

The experience with my former boss stuck with me and has been a great reminder of what I don't want to do with any of my direct reports or the teams I lead. With my current team, I've had to relay difficult news, such as elim-inating the approved back-fill roles we needed, changing the scope of what our team works on, or reporting to another division of the organization. Rather than over-think it, taking too much time to get to the point or not sharing the news at all, I address it head-on. If a change is coming, I tell my team:

- Here is the change
- This is what I thought about it at first and how I reacted
- Here's how I think about it now

Then, I give them time to digest it. (I had that time, so they should get it too.) I provide space for them to ask questions, and we talk about what the news means to all of us. It's not easy, and in some instances, we all may feel crappy about the situation. But it feels a lot better when we know that it's honest and that we're in it together.

This lesson has helped me personally as well. Allen and I have been together for almost ten years, and this lesson is something we both have to work on *all the time.*

I'll say, for example, "I want to go watch Owen play baseball this weekend. That's my truth, but it means I won't be around this weekend to spend time with you. What do we need to talk about in order for me to feel good about going to baseball and for you to have a good weekend as well?" Prior to practicing this lesson, going to Owen's game would have been met with unsaid disappointment and led to resentment on both sides. There were a few times when I didn't express my truth, spent all weekend at the baseball field, and told him to get over it, which was never the right approach.

Another example is when I'd tell Allen I was going to leave the office by five, when I knew, based on my workload and obligations, I wasn't going to leave until six or seven. I knew he wanted me to be home in time to eat dinner with him and the boys, but because I didn't want to disappoint him, I wasn't honest and up front about the reality of the situation. Rather, I'd keep working, watch the clock, send a text now and then to let him know I was getting delayed, until finally, he knew I wasn't going to be home in time, leaving us *both* disappointed in *me*. When I would finally arrive home, I'd feel compelled to create a story around my tardiness to explain why I wasn't home earlier. This almost always led to an argument and hurt feelings.

Once I took this lesson to heart and applied it to both my professional and personal life, I found freedom. In my relationship with my husband, it means I'm committed to speaking the truth *all* of the time, even when it's not easy and when I know disappointment will exist. We both have strong personalities, which means we don't back down. We both can dig our heels in deep. Rather than try to go round and round until one of us "wins" and the other gives up or gives in (the direction where both of our personalities naturally lean), being committed to the truth enables us to deal with the consequences of what's being said, so we can handle it.

Now, it's more of an approach of "This is how it is," and "Are we both prepared to deal with that?" Or: "Does it really cause issues?" and, "If it causes issues, let's talk about it and come to resolution." All of this work still may lead to disappointment, but we have found that being unwilling to speak the truth is usually at the heart of any disagreement, misunderstanding, or miscommunication.

Commit now to speaking the truth and working through the consequences of that with whomever you need to. Again, it's not easy, but it does open the door to what you each need to say and what you need to hear to move forward with each other.

HOW THIS LESSON CAN HELP YOU

You have to feel comfortable telling the truth, even though it's not comfortable. And you have to practice this skill all the time because *radical candor equals freedom.*

Radical candor is freeing because, when you tell the truth, you never have to remember what you said. When you *don't* tell the truth, you're held hostage to that lie. You have to recall the story you've told and the details you've made up. When you tell the truth from the beginning, you don't have to worry about any of that.

Telling the truth is hard, so many people overly compliment instead. Just like too much criticism is problematic, too much praise is too.

In the workplace, some people are overly nice and generous with compliments when reviewing either work quality or what's being produced. If everything is *amazing*, then nothing is amazing. In other words, this makes it difficult to determine what *is* good and what isn't.

That confusion leads to uncertainty.

- Did I not understand the expectation?
- Was I unclear as to what we were supposed to deliver?
- Did I deliver something incredible, or were people too uncomfortable to tell the truth?

If you give feedback and state, "Oh, this is great. Thanks so much for doing that," but in the back of your mind, you're thinking, "This isn't what I need," how do you go back and tell that person what's wrong? You failed to do so when you had the opportunity, and you can't undo that—at least not comfortably. In my experience, delayed feedback is a tough pill to swallow, both for the recipient and the one delivering the critique.

Not giving real feedback in the workplace doesn't help anyone improve—it only helps someone feel better about a situation temporarily. If you want to get a project or presentation moving in the right direction, how are you going to do that if you say everything is great or you don't say anything at all?

If you don't tell the truth, the problem isn't resolved, and you're still in the same situation.

Put yourself in the other person's shoes. If you provide accolades instead of confronting the issue, how does that help the other person? It doesn't.

You must nip the problem in the bud, so it doesn't continue to be a problem as time goes on. Where you came from helped shape who you are, but it's what you do now that determines how others perceive you. When people see that telling the truth and admitting your mistakes is how you operate, they will come to understand you are an honest and accountable person, you possess integrity, and they can trust you. That's what they remember and hold on to, and that's why they'll want to work with you or continue to have a relationship with you.

QUESTIONS TO ASK YOURSELF

As children, we are told to always tell the truth. As adults, we need to be reminded of this lesson from time to time, which means we need a more mature approach and line of questioning to guide us.

Ask yourself:

- What do you know to be true about this situation?
- How do you feel about the situation?
- What do you think about the situation?
- What are you going to say about this situation?
- How are you going to say it?
- How do you show up and speak your truth?
- How do you create an environment where others can do the same?
- What is the best-case scenario if you share this information?
- What is the worst-case scenario?
- How will you navigate the reality that comes with sharing?

Speak the truth (so others can do something productive with it), be receptive of the truth (even if it's hard to hear), and tell things how they are, so others will know where you stand.

This lesson also means you need to be willing to admit your mistakes when you make them. When my brother and I broke my dad's brand-new recliner, it took us *years* to admit it, only to find out when we did, he knew all along.

All those hours going mad, thinking about what I had done, and what he would do if he found out—all that negative energy, and for what? If I had simply told the truth, I wouldn't have gone through so much anguish. It would have been really hard, but imagine how much better I would have felt—for years. Doesn't it, then, make sense to apply that same logic to our adult encounters? Isn't telling the truth the right thing to do, both for them and for *us*?

We've all told lies—we're human. But if we reflect back on those choices and see what we could have done differently, we can see why it's so much simpler to be accountable and tell the truth.

Reflection is the theme of the eighth and final lesson, and true to Dad's form, he had his own special way of saying it: "What have you done for the good of the community today?"

Dad, me, and the recliner

WHAT HAVE YOU DONE FOR THE GOOD OF THE COMMUNITY TODAY?

Years ago, while my dad was still alive, I'd call him every day on my drive home from work to check in. I wanted to see how he was doing and share any news from my day, big or small.

"John Monson speaking," he'd say, even though the trusty flip-phone he kept in the front pocket of whichever collared shirt he was wearing that day had caller-ID.

"Dad, you know it's me," I'd say, shaking my head and smiling. With a chuckle, I'd continue, "What are you doing?"

He'd share a few updates or news of what he'd been working on and then quickly follow with, "What did you do
for the good of the community today, kid?"

It was *the* question he'd ask to kick off our evening
conversation.

Sometimes I'd answer with a story about a big project
that was wrapping up or some new, exciting work I was
starting to plan. On other days, I didn't have much to say.
Maybe, "I had the best lunch," or "I talked to so-and-so,
who I hadn't talked to in a long time."

On the rare occasion, I'd say, "I don't think I did much of
anything today, Dad."

When I said that, I instantly felt like I was in grade school
again, my ponytail bouncing as I bounded down the steps
of the school bus when it dropped me off at the end of
the dirt road that led to the farm. My smile was big, and I
raced toward my dad, who was standing tall with his arms
crossed, outside the Quonset door.

"What did you learn in school today, Marn?" he'd ask, and I'd typically respond with an, "I don't know." He would continue to poke and prod, and I would eventually tell him everything that happened at school.

Even as an adult, Dad never let me off the hook easily. He would say, "Ah, come on. You had to have done something." He'd dig to get the details of important stories, which then led to more conversation.

And on those days when I didn't have much to share, he'd say, "Marn, we all do something for the good of the community, each day."

Of course, he was right. Every day, we do something that impacts the world around us. Most of us are just too busy to notice.

So, I would think about my day and the things I had done. Dad would sit in silence and allow me the space to gather my thoughts. When I was finally ready to share, he was there to listen.

TAKE THE TIME TO REFLECT

Dad's message wasn't philanthropic—it was about reflection. I'm not sure he even knew that, but looking back on those conversations, I now know that's what he meant. When he asked me, "What have you done for the good of the community today?" he wanted me to think about my day and tell him the highlights. He was asking me to reflect.

Not to say Dad wasn't charitable—he was. He did things around town and for others as he determined a need. When he found out our priest didn't have a dishwasher, not only did my dad buy him one, he installed it. And that's just one example. Throughout my life, Dad was very philanthropic and generous.

But this lesson isn't about being charitable. It's about taking the time to think about your day and everything you've done, and the impact those actions have.

Each day, we have the opportunity to impact ourselves or others, positively or negatively. We can do something to improve ourselves, we can do something to harm ourselves, or we can nothing at all. Each day, we have the opportunity to change or to settle for what we have. But if we don't take inventory and the time to reflect on what we've done, we won't have enough information to make decisions about what to do next. Reflection is a way for us to review our actions and make adjustments in order to grow.

People are so busy these days, they don't take time to reflect. I see it in my own work, and I see it in my personal life. I see it in everyone around me who is stressed out: the woman who is trying tirelessly to climb the corporate ladder, the overly stressed entrepreneur, the employee who's stuck in a rut, the anxiety-ridden college kid.

Those in the workforce don't stop to consider if something they developed worked, if they liked it, or if they didn't. Others are too busy trying to do whatever they think they need to accomplish in order to move up in their careers, plowing ahead without reflecting on whether it's all necessary.

Some people find it's easier to go to that next appointment, do the next meeting, put out the next report, go to their kid's game, do this and do that, then rinse and repeat—all because it prevents them from sitting with their own thoughts.

- It's okay to stop for a moment
- It's okay to sit in your own thoughts
- It's okay to feel emotional about what you might be thinking
- It's okay to learn from what you are doing and to grow from it

Intentionally carve out time to reflect, even though it's often difficult to figure out how. Reflecting doesn't have to lead to monumental changes or major life decisions. It's simply giving yourself time to think, and it's one of the greatest gifts you can give to yourself.

If you reflect after having walked away from something, you might decide, "Today is a great day, and I'm pretty darn thankful for that."

Or you might decide, "What the hell am I doing with my life? I need to change something."

If nothing else, reflecting will give you time to think about what you've done, and the resulting feelings have the potential to, ultimately, open doors to gratitude. This is why reflecting is a skill—a "give-me shot" of sorts—you must build, practice, and protect at all costs.

REFLECTION IS A REALITY CHECK

When we reflect, we realize we contribute, achieve, and accomplish more than we think. We're also able to identify something we may want to change. This could be making more time for something or someone, doing more or less, starting something new, or identifying something we want to eliminate.

Daily reflection can provide us with:

- A reality check
- Time for us to recognize or identify something that isn't working for us
- Space for us to appreciate what we've done
- Time to be thankful for what we have and appreciate the life we've created

Taking the time to just be in the moment and reflect on my day, while so simple, is not easy. I struggle with "Get to this; go to that; fix this; do that." I feel life is going by quickly—I think we all do.

So many of us speed through life without looking around to see what we are doing. Then, we're left spinning our wheels, confused as to why we keep repeating the same patterns. When we reflect, we can correct things we're doing that hinder us and live a fuller life.

This is why you need to make space, every day, just to be. To think, without other competing activities or obligations, and reflect on *you*.

I have found I need this lesson more than any of the others because much of my life has been about moving "onward and upward"—I've been very "busy" thinking about the next thing, getting the next job, or completing the next project. So much so, that I know I didn't spend enough time reflecting.

Sometimes, "onward and upward" makes us think we need to do more and causes us to say things like, "I don't have time for this" or "We need to get going." Reflection is powerful because it helps us see the reality of our lives and helps us realize we *do* have the time, and we *don't* have to do more. We can clearly see what's happening and what we may want to change or experience differently.

But regardless of your situation, if you enjoy what you are doing, are contemplating doing something different, or anything in between, reflection (most simply stated) provides you with the time to embrace the decisions you've made, appreciate the situation you've been in, and evaluate how you're going to handle similar instances in the future. That may mean deciding to do something differently or deciding to do nothing at all and just be. Whatever it is, acquiring that clarity is difficult without taking time to reflect.

This doesn't have to be in the form of meditation—this can be time during your morning workout, your commute home, or a few minutes before you go to bed. When you reflect, you can simply think about it, record it, or even write about it. There is no requirement for *how* you reflect, just that you *do*.

My only advice when you start: don't judge—just identify what you're reflecting on. Over time, you can begin to decide what you think about those reflections and what you'll do with them, but don't worry about that right now. This is time for you, so go easy on yourself. No judgment necessary.

HOW THIS LESSON HELPED ME

At times, I have an overflowing plate. I work full-time and have a husband and two children, who have very different activities to attend because they're ten years apart.

For a long time, I didn't listen to this lesson and didn't take time to reflect. That's why I started thinking about writing this book fourteen years ago (before my dad died) and, until now, only wrote a few pieces here and there. Instead of making it a priority and taking time to reflect on why I wanted to write it, I was too busy chasing everything else in my life.

And the book didn't get written, even though it was the one thing I wanted to do.

When I finally took the time to reflect and listen to this lesson, I realized I should have written this book a long time ago. Out of all my dad's sayings, this one is probably my favorite. "What have you done for the good of the community today?" inspired me to reflect on my life and the lessons he taught me throughout the years. This lesson was the catalyst for completing this book. It's what got me writing.

Now, each morning I reflect on my life while working out. It's my time for myself, a time that I make sure to carve out in my day. Without it, I'd go bonkers. Some days, especially on the weekends, I'll ride my Peloton for almost two hours while listening to Dave Matthews Band, removing my hands from the handlebars just long enough to record a voice memo or quickly type some thoughts to myself in a journal app.

Other times, I'll sit alone on my patio and write.

Reflecting has also helped me in business. Once, I was speaking on a professional development panel with a few other colleagues, who were leaders and part of my community group within our office. We were asked to talk about our experiences and how they led us to where we were professionally at that time. This was meant to show how we each took different roads to achieve success.

Everyone in the office was invited to attend. Most were early in their careers.

When the panel began, much of what our chief technology officer shared at the time resonated with me. She has an incredible background and is a talented leader.

She said, "I've always been chasing the next thing."

That hit me hard. *I've* always chased the next thing, and I had never heard anyone else describe their life the same way. Like me, she always chased the next thing—she always focused on the *next* promotion, the *next* opportunity, the *next* thing on her life list, and never stopped to enjoy her accomplishments.

I just ran and ran and ran, thinking I had to do and have more. And I often didn't stop to celebrate once I achieved whatever I was aiming for. I didn't think about what it took to achieve it, what I liked and didn't like about it, or why. I simply got excited for a moment and then moved on to chasing the next thing.

Hearing her make that very pointed statement was a major wake-up call for me. Now, I spend just as much time reflecting on my professional decisions as I do my personal ones.

HOW THIS LESSON CAN HELP YOU

Life is always changing (professionally and personally), and reflecting helps you adjust your decisions in future scenarios. It helps you grow, meet challenges, and make changes when they are warranted.

Staying busy and working constantly is the antithesis of what you need. In order to get ahead, you need to stop working so much and take more time to think about your life. Even when others are competing for your time—and they always will—you need to reflect on what you are doing. Take the time to ask yourself:

- Is this what I want to do?

- Do I enjoy this?
- Am I willing to keep going even though this is hard?
- What truly needs my time and attention?
- Am I celebrating my accomplishments?
- Am I sharing my celebrations with others?

I recently connected with a former member of my team who is incredibly hard working, successful, and bright, but who is struggling. She constantly chases after the next big thing but doesn't make time for reflection. So, my advice to her was to spend time reflecting.

I said to her, "You are working around the clock. Your work has been, and continues to be, your main focus. What are you chasing? Is this what you want? Take the time to think about that. Sit, reflect, and decide what you really want for your career and for your life and how you are going to get it. When you decide that, then you'll know what to chase."

You have to start carving out time for yourself to reflect, otherwise you won't do it. This is the advice I gave my teammate, and it's the advice I remind myself of daily too. I have to intentionally carve out time to reflect, like I did when I talked to my dad on the ride home each night from work—the commute was a time to talk to him and reflect on my day.

Don't wait another day to take time to reflect. Regardless of your age or where you are at in life, start reflecting now. And do it each and every day.

It's not necessary to spend hours each day reflecting. Start with one minute. Set a reminder. Then, sit down and reflect on what you did for the good of the community that day. If you're sitting on the train, driving to or from work, or sitting in the pickup lane waiting for your child after a day at school, remind yourself to reflect. If the only time you have to yourself is in the shower, that's when you should take the time to do it.

QUESTIONS TO ASK YOURSELF

The act of reflection isn't complicated if you carve out the time to do so, and questions are a great tool to use if you're struggling. I use these very simple questions to assist me in daily reflection:

- What happened today (or yesterday)?
- How do I feel about it?
- What do I want to do about it?

I'm glad I've done the things I've done in my life. I don't regret chasing what I desired. I only wish I had carved out more time to reflect and reminded myself to do it, so I could have stayed on track more easily instead of getting fed up with things or staying too busy to enjoy them.

Every day, I miss my dad—and I especially miss those calls on my commute home. But I still hear his voice and his insightful question as if he's still here with me...

"What have you done for the good of the community today, Marn?"

CONCLUSION

I'm very thankful for what my dad has given me. His advice was meaningful and powerful and has shaped my life in more ways than I ever could have imagined.

Even at the end of his life, his actions and example changed me.

My dad's last days were spent in a fairly large hospital room in Denver, Colorado, after being transferred there from the ICU in North Platte, Nebraska. He had been out running errands with my mom when he became light headed and backed into a parked car in the parking lot, a red flag that his oxygen levels were too low.

He got to the hospital in Denver and was confined to a bed on the far end of the room near a small window and a semi-recliner chair where my mom or I would take turns sleeping in overnight to stay with him. My dad died in November, during football season. Like any die-hard Nebraska football fan, which my dad was, we watched games on the big screen TV on the wall of his hospital room.

Because he was dying of pulmonary fibrosis, which is a hardening of the lungs, he required a full-face oxygen mask to breathe and would have suffocated if his oxygen levels dropped too low. To this day, the medical community isn't sure what causes the disease. Some refer to it as "farmer's lung," which results from farmers spending a lot of time sweeping grain bins and inhaling dust and other particles, which my dad had done many times. Others wonder if it can be influenced by smoking, which my dad had done for many years before quitting cold turkey almost twelve years before he died. The cause didn't matter at that point. He had it. He was sick. And he was dying.

As my dad drew closer to death, the clinical team couldn't oxygenate him enough through the mask.

He was struggling to breathe while I sat in the corner, desperate to help him and knowing I couldn't. My mom was standing up, probably feeling the same way.

The doctor said, "We have three options. Number one: We can put a breathing tube in you, which would mean you'd be unconscious. It will keep you alive, but I don't know if we'll ever be able to get you off it. Number two: We can make you comfortable and let nature take its course. Or number three: We can keep doing what we're doing and see if it gets better."

At that point, my dad had been fighting to stay alive for almost three weeks. The sparkle in his bright blue eyes had all but vanished. Exhausted, he could hardly keep his eyes open. But after a few moments of what looked like he was collecting his own thoughts, he turned his head slightly toward the doctor and asked, "What were the choices again?"

After the doctor repeated them, we all knew the third option wasn't viable. He'd been in option three for some time, and it wasn't working. To continue would mean suffering. That left the other two.

Dad, who could hardly breathe and hardly speak, looked up again to the doctor, almost like a child looking upward toward a parent, and asked, "What would you do?"

That moment was so powerful for me.

I'd always known my dad to have an opinion on everything, to state it and make a decision. I never had to wonder if he *had* an opinion or what it was, but at that moment, when my dad's opinion mattered most, he asked the doctor what *he* would do. At the time, it made me feel sad because I thought it showed weakness in my dad.

I now know differently. Asking for advice and then taking it isn't a sign of weakness; it's the ultimate show of strength. When you ask for help, you get what you need. Here was a man who had given others advice all his life, and now, in his darkest hour, when he needed critical advice, he was strong enough to ask for it.

The doctor said, "John, I can't do that. I can't tell you what to do. You're going to have to make that decision for yourself." But after a pause, the doctor looked at my dad again, placed his hand on my dad's forearm, and said, "You should do what's best for *you*."

Dad shifted his head back to center, stared directly forward, and didn't say anything. Tears ran down my mom's face. Tears ran down mine. We all sat there staring at my dad while he stared straight ahead.

Then, without saying a word, my dad slowly lifted his right hand, the hand closest to where the doctor stood, and for all of us to see, firmly lifted two fingers, indicating choice number two: make him comfortable and let nature take its course. The movement was intentional and deliberate, just like everything Dad had always done.

So many thoughts were going through my head at that moment, but there was one I remember distinctly: "He's choosing to die right now. This is it."

He didn't want my mom and me to have to make a horrible decision, one where there seemed to be no good options. He didn't want us to have to live with that, especially if he was put on a ventilator and couldn't come off it—where we'd have to decide if and when to pull the plug. He loved us and my siblings, who couldn't be there, too much to put that burden on any of us. He made the decision on his own, so we didn't have to.

Here was this man who had given me so much incredible advice throughout my entire life, and it only seemed fitting that he go out *his* way—that he was strong, even in his weakest moment. That he made the choice how to die.

Once he decided to let nature take its course and after the nurses pumped him full of morphine, I laid down next to him in the hospital bed, put my head between his arm and his shoulder, and said, "Thank you, thank you" over and over again. "Thank you for everything that you've given me. Thank you for everything that you taught me. I will never forget. I love you, Dad."

I didn't say anything after that.

I just lay there until he took his last breath.

DAD'S INFLUENCE ON OTHERS

The church was packed at Dad's funeral; some stood outside or in the basement because there simply wasn't enough room in the nave. And so many of those people drove to the cemetery to honor Dad and to support us.

The night before his funeral, I was in a fog when we arrived home after the traditional Catholic rosary service to find our entire living room full of people who had brought over food. Some of these people included friends I hadn't seen in many years.

Darcy was one of them. We'd grown up together, but after what seemed like a twenty-year absence, I just shook my head and said, "Oh my God…what are you doing here?"

She said, "A few years ago, when I was going through my divorce, I came to one of the high school games, and your dad talked to me. He was always the nicest man. And he stood there and listened and talked me through what I was dealing with. He had great advice for me."

So many people told me stories after Dad died about how incredibly nice he was or what he did to help them. How he offered advice that improved their lives.

I knew Dad's advice had impacted my life, but until that time, I had no idea how much Dad's advice had impacted the entire community. Outside the church following his funeral, as well as during the walk back to my vehicle after the burial service, I saw my former classmates, some of whom I hadn't seen since high school graduation. Their presence was felt, even if we didn't speak to each other that day. I know they were there to support me, but I knew they were *mostly* there because my dad influenced them in some way, just like his lessons had influenced me.

The lessons presented in this book, lessons my dad taught me and others, are core lessons that speak to all people. And even though I've heard them all my life and have seen them in action, I've steered away from them at times. To this day, I still have to remind myself to think about these lessons from time to time because that's what it takes to implement them into your life. You have to learn the lessons and then practice them daily.

No one has the answers to everything. We all face struggles and have difficulty making decisions. When you find yourself struggling, remember to return to the meaningful and powerful advice presented in this book. No matter what you're dealing with, there's a lesson to help you get through it.

Here's a quick summary guide:

Lesson 1: Be Proud of Where You Came From
Lesson 2: Start with the Give-Me Shots
Lesson 3: Know the Rules of the Game
Lesson 4: Work While Others are on Break
Lesson 5: Don't Bite Off More Than You Can Chew
Lesson 6: Always Find a Win-Win Solution
Lesson 7: Tell the Truth, and You Never Have to Remember What You Said
Lesson 8: What Have You Done for the Good of the Community Today?

REFLECT AND TAKE ACTION

Now that you've read the advice my dad gave me, what it meant to me while growing up, and how it still has meaning for me today, take Lesson 8 to heart and start to reflect on your own life.

Maybe, like me, you've forgotten some good advice over the years. That's completely understandable. Now is the time to revisit and reconnect with the advice you've received, both in this book and beyond. What sage advice has been passed down to you from loved ones? Have you thought about it? It's right there in front of you, just like the pages of this book.

Ask yourself:

- Where have you found advice?
- Who gave you the advice?
- How have you implemented the advice into your life?
- How did the advice positively impact your life?
- Are you continuing to apply the advice right now? If not, why?

Whether you commit to some of the lessons I've provided in this book, a few, or just one, think about how the lesson(s) could positively impact your life. Then, revisit the respective lesson(s) from time to time.

I revisit these lessons over and over again. Though I've heard them my entire life, I have to consciously think about them. You probably will have to think about them too. But the beautiful thing is that as soon as you identify the lessons that matter to you and that will have a positive impact on your life, you will take a step forward in the right direction.

Now that you know the lessons, it's time to execute.

What are you waiting for?

If you need additional help to understand and implement the lessons, need leadership or team coaching, or if your organization is looking for someone to speak to or come in to develop large groups of people, reach out to me at *www.marneyandes.com.*

In the spirit of my dad and with words he'd often say, I'll say this to all of you: "Just give me a buzz. I'm happy to help."

ACKNOWLEDGMENTS

I have a number of people to thank for making this book possible.

My husband, Allen, who didn't blink an eye when I said I wanted to write a book, unconditionally supported me throughout the process, and will continue to practice these lessons with me, here on out.

My boys, Owen and Brody, who understood when I was "working while others were on break," were willing to wait for me, and gave me the space I needed to write.

My mom, Lynda, who helped me describe people, places, or situations shared in the book, as needed. Eternally a proud mom, her praise along the way kept me believing this book was worthy.

My siblings, Cris and Mandy, for being my partners in crime in many of the experiences mentioned in this book, being excited for me when they found out about the book, and then doing what we all do best together: "one upping" each other about what would have been better titles for the lessons.

My aunt, Karen, who brainstormed some of the best advice themes with me and confirmed the value of advice we've all been handed down over the years.

My ex-husband, Scott, who continues to be a friend and part of my journey.

My friends, Lisa Woods and Sheryl Gurrentz, who inspire me to take risks and always hold space for me to share and learn.

My long-time colleague, Dan Morris, who, so many years ago, took me on the "tour of Colorado" and fostered my love of helping teachers use technology.

My friends, at East Central BOCES, especially Anita Burns, Sharon Daxton-Vorce, and Lorie Coonts, who always thought of me for new projects and in turn, helped me build a successful consulting business.

My mentor, Allison Velez, who has always trusted me to do the work and provided me opportunities from which I could practice, learn, and grow.

My colleagues, Kathy Kelley and Susan Alonzi, who have shaped my views and approaches to supporting leaders.

My teammate, Jon Folkestad, who doesn't realize it but is one of my core sounding boards. Your approach and way of navigating how we support leaders and teammates is special.

My teammate, Julie Applegate, who has ridden this wave of leadership development with me over the years and now teaches me more about it than I have ever taught her. Thank you for modeling the heart that goes into supporting others.

My teammate, Tom McFaul, who's never-ending focus on ensuring the work that we do, makes an impact, continues to influence how I think about and engage in this life work. I'm so grateful we met in that campus learning lab.

To all of the other teammates whom I've led, worked with, and have been influenced by, thank you for the perpetual reminder that the journey of helping everyone do their best work, while sometimes challenging, is worth it.

Thank you to the community of Wallace, Nebraska, where it all started and was fostered; you will forever hold a special place in my heart.

My colleague, Heather Hanson Wickman, who listened to my book idea and connected me to the right people to get it started.

My friend, Lynn Gangone, who, when asked to write the foreword to this book, didn't hesitate. Thank you for the kind words and ongoing support.

My photographer, Megan Anderson, who has incredible knack for capturing the real me in headshots and who helped ensure the old photos with my dad looked great for print.

Thank you to Derrick Hall, Matt Blumberg, and Julie Love for taking the time to read, review, and provide such thoughtful endorsements.

And to everyone at Scribe Media for believing that this was a book worth writing and that many others would benefit from reading. Thank you to Libby Allen, who kept us on pace, Barbara Boyd, who provided editing expertise throughout and special touches in final review, and Rachael Brandenburg, who captured the essence of this book in a meaningful cover design. A special thanks to Lisa Caskey, who (through deep conversations, laughter, and tears) helped me bring these stories to life—what a beautiful friendship we've created through this process.

ABOUT THE AUTHOR

Marney Andes is a born-and-bred farm girl from Wallace, Nebraska. A consultant, educator, and entrepreneur, she has dedicated her career to supporting teams and individuals as they develop and grow.

Her experience in performance consulting and leadership development spans a wide range of industries, including technology, healthcare, education, and nonprofit. A college basketball player and former Mrs. America, Marney is the founder of Project Aspire, a nonprofit created to support women in their pursuit of higher education and leadership opportunities.

Marney holds a master's in information and learning technologies from the University of Colorado Denver and currently resides outside of Denver with her husband, Allen, and her two sons, Owen and Brody.

CPSIA information can be obtained
at www.ICGtesting.com
Printed in the USA
LVHW101030070922
727788LV00008B/51

9 781544 518695